My First Book of Magic

"Real magic but more importantly, real wisdom. A great introduction to the magical arts for any age, but particularly delightful for kids starting upon the path. 'My First Book of Magic' gives a solid foundation to the reader." - Christopher Penczak, Author of 'The Inner Temple of Witchcraft' and 'Sons of the Goddess'.

"Magic is like an adventure but is not a game. It teaches secrets about yourself and the powers of nature. It teaches you to enjoy being part of everything around you. This book is meant for children, but it's must for any passionate pagan and magician." - Jorge Nájera, Director of Studies, Fraternidad del Círculo Dorado.

"This delightful book was written for children but is actually for all ages.If you have have ever had an interest in magic, and wish to know more this is the book for you. It is a very enjoyable and informative primer packed with information." - Betty deMaye-Caruth PhD, RN, CHTP

"This little book of magic for pagan children gives an insider's view of what magic really is and how it is done with love, ethics and joy. It is just the thing for burgeoning minds that are opening to the wider universe and its unseen inhabitants, led by the most revered teacher of the Western Magical Tradition."- Caitlín Matthews, author of 'Singing the Soul Back Home'.

"I knew that something was calling to me when I was a child, something both old and evergreen. I wish I'd found 'My First Book of Magic' as it would have saved me some scrapes and scares. It would also have set me sooner on the path that I follow today. If you have a child in your life that has the look of the far memory in their eyes, gift them with this guide. If you remember the child you were, read this book and reopen the gates of your wonder." - Ivo Dominguez Jr., author of 'Keys to Perception'.

My First Book of Magic

Dolores Ashcroft-Nowicki

With illustrations by Carl Ashcroft

Megalithica Books

Stafford England

Editor: Louise Coquio
Layout: Storm Constantine
Cover Art: Carl Ashcroft
Cover Design: Danielle Lainton
Interior illustrations by Carl Ashcroft

ISBN: 978-1-912241-10-1
MB0202

Set in Book Antiqua

A Megalithica Books Publication
An imprint of Immanion Press
info@immanion-press.com
http://www.immanion-press.com

Contents

Dedication

This book is dedicated to every child who reads it.

It was written for YOU, so just write your name in the space below.

To

_____

With love and good wishes from

Dolores

This book is also dedicated to

My daughter, Tamara, and my son, Carl,
Who supported me through the devastating year
of 2018

Foreword

J. H. Brennan

Back in the 1980s, I wrote my first series of fantasies for children. They took the form of novelty items known as gamebooks and I was a long way from taking them seriously. I churned them out at the rate of one a month, let my imagination run riot and entertained myself hugely without so much as a nod towards literature's demands for characterisation or plot. My expectations for them were low and while they sold well enough, I knew they were just part of a fad that was likely to run its course in a couple of years, then disappear from the marketplace.

And I was right. The kids who once went wild for gamebooks discovered computer gaming, publishers decided gamebooks were history and the genre shrank to miniscule proportions. I turned my mind to other things.
Then, thirty years later, something odd happened. With the internet a ubiquitous fact of life, I began to get emails from men and women who had played my gamebooks as children and were now searching for second-hand copies so their own children could play them in their turn. Some of them were kind enough to say my work had helped them through a difficult childhood. Some of them said I had changed their lives.

I found it hard to believe, but as more and more emails arrived, I was forced to accept that some children's books are actually like that. They have an influence far beyond anything their authors expected or intended.

I suspect *My First Book of Magic* is such a book.

Like Dion Fortune in another era, Dolores Ashcroft-Nowicki is a high-grade psychic who has dedicated her life to esoteric study and practice. She has no 'day job.' Her time is totally devoted to an ongoing investigation of the ancient wisdom. As a result, she has accumulated a breadth and depth of knowledge that is almost unimaginable.

Throughout her long life, she has generously shared that knowledge through a series of books, many of which have become classics in their field. But of all the literary works she has produced, I venture to suggest none is more important than the present unassuming opus. For here, with an extraordinary degree of sensitivity, Dolores has elected to undertake that most difficult of tasks, the esoteric education of children.

Nor has she been content to confine herself to the basic principles of practical magic, simplified to match a child's understanding. From the very beginning, she has been careful to concentrate on the ethics of magical practice – a subject sadly lacking in many adult books on the subject.The result is something unique – a comprehensive understanding of a subject of perennial fascination to the youngest of our younger generation. It is for this reason that I suspect the work will gain an influence far more profound than its author imagines.

And an influence that is well deserved.

Herbie Brennan
Author of *Fairy Wars* (New York Times Best Seller)

Preface

I have wanted to write this book for a long time simply because there is little available to teach pagan children about their religion and how to work magic. I was lucky and had parents and a grandmother who taught me from my earliest days. But though we are no longer seen as outcasts for being pagan-minded there is still a lot of prejudice when it comes to teaching pagan ways to children.

However, at 89 I am old enough to stick my neck out and take any criticisms that come my way, and I am expecting there will be quite a few. I have taken care to make the instructions understandable and fun. In many ways they resemble the instructions I was given from five years onward.

At the moment, there is little in the way of Pagan Belief Teachings for children to get to know and understand. Here in England, fewer and fewer people are going to church of any denomination so children are growing up with little or no idea of there being something greater than ourselves, be it a great teacher like Jesus, a mystic like Gautama, a godform such as Shiva, or the Moon Mother and Her Horned Lord.

We all need something to believe in, something to give us hope of a future with some semblance of peace. Pagan practice may not be right for everyone, but it does at least invoke a spirit of community and togetherness. Along with the knowledge that we are not the only beings to inhabit this earth.

Dolores Ashcroft-Nowicki

With that in mind I am sending this book out into the world and hoping it will serve some purpose.

I would like to say a big thank you to Immanion Press for giving me this opportunity and for their patience in waiting for the long overdue manuscript. Thanks also to my dearest long-time friend and prolific author Herbie Brennan, who wrote the foreword. More than anyone I know he understands the minds and hearts of children and how amazingly bright they are.

Lastly, a big thank you to my son Carl for the illustrations: you caught just the look I was hoping for. It was great to work with you, let's do it again soon.

Dolores Ashcroft-Nowicki
Jersey, May 2019

Alphabet for Small Witches.

A is for Angels, who guard me at night.

B is for Bonefire, a magical sight.

C is the Cup that is shared by us all

D is for Dance, when the pipers do call

E is for Easter, the time of the hare

F is for Fairy, if you tease them – beware

G is for Goddess, the Mother of all

H is the Hunter, so strong and so tall

I is for Incense, slow-burning and sweet

J is the Joy that we share when we meet

K is the Kiss twixt the Hunter and Maid

L is the Log on the Yule fire laid

M is for Mabon, when the Goddess descends

N is for Need-fire, to the cattle it tends

O is for Owl, such a magical bird

P is for Pixie, who is seen but not heard.

Q is a Quill pen, only used by a few

R is for Ritual to make things come true,

S is a Symbol with something to say

T is a Talisman, for luck, so they say

U is for Unicorn, seen from afar

Dolores Ashcroft-Nowicki

V is for Venus, the bright Evening Star

W is for Wicca, the wise ones of old

X marks the spot of a treasure, I'm told

Y is for Yuletide and St Nicholas' Day

Z ends our song as we go on our way

Chapter One
What IS Magic?

Magic is something that's all around us, but we don't call it magic because we see and use it every day. We are so used to turning on a TV, using a phone, a car or a computer that we forget that three hundred years ago those things would have been viewed as magic, and that meant that you could have been imprisoned for using them. People then were frightened of things they didn't understand and, even today, some people still are. Things are better now, and we know that not everyone lives in the same way, or believes in the same thing, but as 'magical people' we still have to be careful how we do things and what we talk about. We have to keep certain things secret unless you are with other magical people.

So, almost all of the things you know and use every day would have been seen as magic once upon a time. In another hundred years we might be able to spend holidays on the moon or even Mars. We might even have airports where you could step into something like an elevator and two minutes later step out into Australia. We may have robot servants who will take children to school, do the shopping, clean the house and walk the dog. We would call that magic today but in one hundred years' time, it could be something everyone uses.

Human beings like to invent things and they have been doing it ever since someone found out how to make fire by rubbing sticks together in a certain way. Magic is something that works in a way we don't always understand. *Yet.* But we'll figure it out eventually, then it won't be magical anymore, but something else will take its place.

We all have a magical power inside us, it's called imagination. Some people call it 'daydreaming' but, whatever you call it, you need to have it if you want to work magic. When you think about something you want really hard, so hard you can almost touch it, see it, even taste it , then that *something* 'feels' your thought and tries very hard to get to you, because it wants to be with you as much as you want to have it. Sometimes it does get to you and sometimes it doesn't. It's all in the way you think or daydream. Because, to make one thing happen, a lot of other things have to move around too so that you can get what you want. This takes time and people get impatient and stop 'dreaming'. If that happens, the thing you want stops trying to get to you. Think of it this way:

Say you would like a pair of new shoes, you know the kind of shoe, the colour, and the size and you think about it a lot. It is close to your birthday and your grandmother says she will buy them for you - so your magical wish is on its way. The day before your birthday you and your grandmother set out to buy the shoes. The first few shops don't have the kind you want, but you keep trying, though it is tiring walking around. In the very last shop, you see the shoes you want, in the right colour and the right size_but, *someone else is trying them on and it's the only pair in your size.* You now have a problem. You have been working magic to get these shoes but now it looks as if your magic has failed, or has it?

Using magic means you are responsible for what happens when it works. You should never deliberately set out to harm other people. Always think about what you want to do or have, very carefully and make sure no one gets hurt. What you want may already belong to someone else who treasures it. Your 'magic' may mean them losing it or it might be stolen and sold - eventually it may come to you, but by causing sadness to the person who owned it first.

Magic is a serious business and nothing like Aladdin's genie, or Cinderella's godmother. Using magic means doing things for the right reason, not just because you want something. If you do, the power might turn around and cause trouble for *you.* So, let's look at the shoe situation again:

You want the shoes, but the other person looks very happy with them. You have spent a lot of time thinking about those shoes and you really, really want them, but can you let the other person buy them, can you give them up because it is the nice thing to do? Can *you* be a 'Fairy Godmother' and let that other 'Cinderella' have the shoes?

If you can't let them go, the other person may find the

shoes are not comfortable when she tries to walk in them. She may look at another pair and decide to buy them instead. Your wish to have those shoes is so strong it has altered the fit of the shoes and made her feet feel hurt when walking in them. Your magic has worked, and you have the shoes, but after you have worn them for a while, they might begin to pinch *your* toes! What happened to the other person is happening to you. This kind of thing happens when magic has been used in the wrong way. Let's go back to when you were in the shop. You see how happy the other person is in the shoes and decide that you will look for something else and you send a '*happy wish*' to the person wearing them. Suddenly, that person sees another pair of shoes she likes even better and changes her mind and buys them instead, so you get the pair she doesn't want anymore. You get your wish; the shoes go home with you. You have worked a small magic, but more importantly you have worked it so that both you *and* the other person both got what you wanted. You have learned the first and most important rule of magic. It goes like this:

- And it harm none -

Good magic teaches you to think about other people; about their feelings, hopes, and dreams. Always begin by asking yourself; '*will this cause trouble for anyone else?*' Of course, you are going to make mistakes and do things wrong- that is how you learn- by making mistakes and remembering not to repeat them.

In past times magic *was* sometimes used to cause harm which is why some people still see magic as being bad. But now it is slowly beginning to be seen as something special, that can be used in good ways.
Although being a witch is not against the law, as it was in

the old days, there will always be people who think the ancient craft is evil and make life difficult for you. When you are older and stronger you can deal with such people. When you are young you are vulnerable and people, other children and even teachers can be cruel in their words and actions. I learned this the hard way when I was young, and people were still afraid of such things.

There are a lot of people who don't know or care about magic and think it's silly to believe in it. But if you are reading this book you are *not* one of those people, there is something inside you that makes you think in a different way. Maybe your parents think differently as well and want you to know and understand what that difference is and how it can be used.

As you get older, you may want to know more about magic or – to give it another name – the occult, a word that simply means "hidden". Or you may find other interests and follow a different path. The world needs people who care about it, whatever their beliefs and interests might be. All beliefs and traditions are important to those who use them and should be respected.

Everyone is born with different talents: for some its science, or medicine, being an astronaut, playing football or tennis or becoming a film star. Some people want to know about ideas, and ways of doing things that are very very old. Magical things. It may be the reason why you are reading this book.

People are special in different ways, they may sing, play an instrument, do complicated sums in their heads, invent things, fly planes, space ships, sail boats and all sorts of wonderful things. Other people are special *inside* themselves and they are the ones who are drawn to magic. There is something special in everyone. They just have to find it. Hopefully you will find out if you are magically special by reading this book.

When you make a wish, or work a spell, the thoughts and ideas inside your head make pictures. Sometimes the pictures are so strong they become a daydream and you can see or feel yourself actually having what you wish for. You know what colour it is, how it feels in your hand or being where you can see it. The thing to remember is that thoughts and daydreams are *real* inside your head, but if you want them to be real *outside* your head, and in the world, you have to work a kind of magic. Thoughts are made of the energies inside your head. We have lots of that energy, and we can learn to use it, but it takes time. This is where that first and most important rule of magic I already told you about comes in, and it *must* be obeyed. When you are older and doing grown up magic it is even more important, so I will say it again: *'And it harm none'* means exactly what it says.

Now we have to go back to the first question and ask: 'What *is* magic?'

We have looked at what was believed to be magical long ago, but what is seen as magical right now? We see films with wonderful special effects and read stories about shape shifters, and people who can teleport from one place to another. But can such things be real?

Magic is about understanding the *Laws of the Universe* and learning to use them. We are just beginning to know about these laws so we don't always know how they work or what we can do with them. But we can learn to use those special *daydreams,* and how to make the pictures in our heads so real they can't do anything else but come true.

Everything begins as a thought or a dream. Everyone has dreams but - and it's a *big* but - not all of them come true. Why? Because most people think they will always be just a dream and don't bother to try to make them come true. They don't want to make the effort it takes; they just want a Disney type of magic to happen without them doing anything about it.

People go to university to study how to be doctors, scientists, farmers, artists, musicians and lots of other things. It takes years to be really good at the subject you are studying. Real magic takes same kind of hard work and, unless you know that, you'll never be a real magician, or witch or wizard. So again, what is magic? It is being able to 'dream' an idea in your head and making it real. Disney Magic is make-believe, real magic takes skill, patience, and belief in yourself. I will teach you some old songs that are sung at certain times of the year and which can draw other beings like fairies, gnomes and elementals closer to you. You may not always see them, but you can feel when they are near.

Some people are born witches, some make themselves witches by hard work. It can be in your blood, your family, your ancestry, if it's there it will show itself at some time in your life. You *can* learn to be a witch but being born into a family of them is better. But remember, there will always be some people who are afraid of magic and of anyone who uses it or even talks about it too much. So, you should be careful who you talk to. Of course, your parents probably gave you the book so they will talk to you about it and answer your questions. But one of the first things you learn is this.... Read, Learn, Practice, but keep Silent outside of your family.

I will show you how to know about, and to make, magic.

What it can be used for, and how. I will tell you about the seasons of the year and the special days in each one. I will teach you about magical creatures like fairies, elementals and spiritual beings like dryads and devas. You will learn to make magical things like wands and cups, swords (*make believe ones until you're old enough to use real ones*), pentacles and robes. It's going to be rather like being a Girl Guide or a Boy Scout only *magical*. Rituals are special meetings and older witches do a lot of them, but I have made some easier ones you can do on your own, or with friends who think like you.

You will learn to make spells, keep a magical diary of the things you learn and do, and how important it is to keep secrets from people that you do not know well and who may not understand what you do. I'll show you how to create a special helper called a familiar, that no one can see except you. Familiars are very good at keeping away things like nightmares and shadows that hide under the bed, or in dark cupboards at night. Some of them can tell you stories to help you sleep, and often go into your dreams with you. We are going to have a lot of fun together so turn the page and let's begin.

Chapter Two
What is a Witch? Rules for Witches And the Magical Name

The word 'witch' has many meanings. We don't know exactly how the word began but most believe it comes from an old English word 'wicca' meaning wise. Where it came from is not as important as how it came to mean someone who works 'magic' in a bad way. Most fairy tales show them as being old, ugly, with a big nose, a hairy chin, and warts. But though witches grow old like everyone else, many of them are young and pretty, some are older and more like grannies and aunties.

A witch is someone who believes that there are other kinds of beings who share the world with us. Fairies, gnomes, undines (the real name for mermaids) and dryads or tree spirits. They believe in the real kind of magic, not the kind you read in stories, or see in films like Cinderella and Snow White, but the kind that means understanding how the four elements of earth, fire, air and water work, and how they can be friendly to those who believe in them. Witches take part in festivals that are often over a thousand years old, because they know those are special times when it is easier to keep the four elements in balance. They know about herbs; which can help sick people, and which are poisonous if eaten. But, in the past, ordinary people had forgotten things like that, so they were frightened of those who did know. They believed witches flew in the air on broomsticks (like Harry Potter in the film.) They thought that witches took off all their clothes and danced under the moon to make people they didn't like become sick, but there are many people who are not witches who do things even worse to people they don't like.

There are good people, bad people and people who are sort of in the middle, and witches are no different. What you are going to learn will hopefully, make you a good person who knows about the old ways like spells, herbs, and the special ways of dancing that makes things happen. But no, you won't be able to fly on a broomstick. I'm sorry about that, but if you want to fly you have to take a plane! But you can learn to do a magical dance, sing a spell, honour the old ways and work real magic in a good way.

A witch believes that there are great powers that we call *earth, air, fire* and *water*; they have special names that you will learn about. A witch knows that there *are* such things as *sylphs, salamanders, gnomes,* and *undines,* but they don't have forms or bodies as we have unless we lend them some of our energy. Their own forms are rather like dreams.

Some people say if you are a witch you can't believe in

God or Jesus, but will tell you how Jesus fed five thousand people on a few fishes and a couple of loaves of bread, or that he made blind people see and lame people walk. They will say that he worked miracles – remember the word miracle means the same as magic – it makes something that seems impossible really happen. So perhaps Jesus actually worked magic of the good kind.

Some people believe that only girls can be witches and call boys who work magic wizards. But the word witch can fit both boys and girls. Wizard is a name given to boys or men who work in special ways. Very often they are what we call alchemists, or they are teachers who take on students, and sometimes they have special and important work to do. When a witch becomes really bad, they are often called sorcerers. From time to time you may read or hear the word 'sorcerer'. You may have heard it in a film, such as the Harry Potter movies, or *Lord of the Rings* or *The Hobbit*. You might have wondered what the difference is between a witch and a sorcerer since they both use magic. Now when someone uses magic for a *long* time it might begin to make them feel very powerful inside. It doesn't happen right away… but over the years that person might get to like being powerful and making others do what they want them to do, not always nice things.

This happened to Voldemort in the Potter books, and the wizard Saruman in *Lord of the Rings*. They began to change people into 'monsters' and send them out to hurt others, cause damage and destroy things people loved. Such people do this because it makes them feel strong and powerful, like a bully in the playground. Being strong and powerful is not bad in itself but if it means making people do things against their will, then the wizard becomes a sorcerer, and their magic becomes dark and evil.

Most people have a little magical power in them but
sometimes you are born with more than usual, especially
if your parents believe in magic. Sometimes it's one of
your grand-parents. The talent for magic can be inherited,
like red hair, blue eyes, or being left-handed. It can take
time to make itself felt, sometimes even an adult suddenly
discovers there is a 'hidden' *witchiness* inside them.

If a group of witches meet regularly, we use the word
'coven' to describe them. It has the same meaning as *'a
group of friends who enjoy playing or working together'*.
However, some witches prefer to work alone. That is
your choice. When you are older you might be invited to
join a coven. There will be a ceremony, rather like a
christening, and you will be able to choose a name to be
used when working with the group. Think about that
name for a while. Don't be in a hurry. Look at the
meaning of it - does it suit you? Does it 'say' something
about you?

Many people choose very old names that are seldom used
now. The internet, or books on the meaning of names, can
give you a list of meanings of old-fashioned names and
from different countries. Look around and find a name
that feels right. It should say something about you as a
person. You might even find your own ancestors had
similar names and it is a nice thing to do to use one of
them. Verity, for instance, is an old name and its meaning
has to do with truth, or something that is real. Dorcas is
another very old name and means gazelle or young deer.
Boys could choose a name from myth, such as Gwion
(gwee-on) or Orion, or the name of a warrior like Achilles,
Gawain or Bran. Remember, this name is used when
working in your group. It is not the same as the really
special name you use when making magic on your own.
So, you have a magical name, which only you know, and

a group name used by those you work with. This may not happen until you are older, but it is something to think about and prepare for.

Most witches refer to the Earth we live on as the *Earth Mother*. She feeds us, gives us trees, flowers, fruit, water, and the beautiful things around us. Many people do not think about her and leave rubbish around, especially plastic, and sharp things that can cause serious harm. If you work magic out of doors, always clear up after yourself, put rubbish in a bag and take it back to put in the garbage. Don't leave broken bottles around or empty Coke tins, plastic bottles, because small animals and insects like bees and butterflies, dormice and voles can crawl inside and get stuck.

If you find a snare or trap of some kind disarm it but be careful how you do it. Bury it and put a stone on top. Above all, use fire with utmost care and only if with someone older. Be sure embers are well and truly put out, leaving no sparks. Always surround a fire with stones to keep it in bounds. Remember to shut farm gates so animals don't wander. If using private ground, make sure you have permission. Always let owners know when you're leaving and thank them.

Just as ordinary people have laws and rules, witches have them as well. I have already told you the most important one – '*And it harm none*' – but there are others, which must always be obeyed:

★ You should never cause hurt, distress, or kill another life form with the intent to do magical work.
★ You keep silent about your work with your coven and do not give out names or meeting times. The only time to do this would be if another/older member of the coven hurt, mistreated or touched you

in a way that made you frightened. Then go to your parents, another relative or an older sibling, or a teacher straight way.

★ You should not reveal your coven name to anyone *outside the group*. Your own magical name is something you keep to yourself alone. If you reveal it by mistake, discard it and choose a new one.

★ Respect those above you in rank and serve them at the feasts. Your turn will come.

★ Do not seek power for its own sake. Those best suited to use power are those who don't really want it.

★ Honour the Earth Mother and care for her creatures, as described earlier in this chapter.

★ Keep your tools, robes and other magical equipment clean and well hidden – do not hand them around or show them off.

★ Always ask permission if you want to touch or handle tools that belong to another witch, even a member of your own family.

★ Wash your hands before using your tools. They are empowered and that power can be lessened if touched with unclean hands.

★ As a witch you are an upholder of the honour of all witches. *Your behaviour reflects on them* so keep that in mind.

★ Remember, you are responsible for the outcome of your magical actions.

★ Do not look down on another person's religion. To believe in a *power for good* that is greater than yourself is the first step to wisdom.

★ When working with other people try to keep everything on a friendly basis. Sometimes in magical work emotions can get out of hand. Tantrums have no place in magical work.

Finally let me tell you what magic is *not*. It is not about having power over people. If that is what you think, you are not going to be able to use magic in the right way. It is not for showing off to friends; the fewer people who know what you do or what you are, the better. While it's important to enjoy working magic and the company of those you might work with, it is *not* just for 'fun'. Magic is a serious study, and as you get older you will find it has many levels and each level has something to offer, challenge or puzzle you.

Magic is *not* a game. It is a way of life that goes back thousands of years and in many forms - it is a set of beliefs, which we call a 'belief system'. In modern terms, it is in many ways equivalent to physics, as it extends your understanding far beyond this planet, solar system, galaxy and even dimensions. Those are big words but not too big for you to read about, ask about, and question older people about them.

Magic is an adventure waiting to happen, but it will only give you as much as you are willing to put into it. It may be that after a while you will find it is not for you. That's alright, your life is yours to do with as you want. It can lead you into deeper things as you grow older. But whatever you decide is up to you, just don't treat it as a game - it isn't! It is a way of living and experiencing things in all sorts of new ways.

Magic also means treating all life as being worthy of respect, and that includes the earth itself. I have a friend who is of the First Nation People[1]. Every morning he touches the earth and says, 'Good morning, my Mother,' then he looks up to the sky and says, 'Good Morning my Father.' I think that is a lovely way to begin the day.

Dolores Ashcroft-Nowicki

1. It was once, until lately, the custom to refer to people of Native American descent as 'Red Indians'. This is not polite and is considered insulting to those referred to as such. You should refer to them either as Native American or as a member of their particular tribe, such as Sioux or Apache or Navaho. Collectively these tribes are known as First Nation People. They were certainly in America long before the Europeans.

Chapter Three
Magic Tools and How to Make Them
(Part One)

Now is the time to make your first magical tools and learn not just *how* to make them, but to name them and bless them and make them ready to use. There is a magical power inside all of us, but most of the time we don't know it or understand it. If we keep our interest in magic, the power inside us will grow with us. If we lose interest it will just remain quiet. But if you let the power grow it will need to be made useful so it can be used with care and attention to detail.

Let's look at the kind of tools a witch needs:

The four main tools are: *the Wand, the Cup, the Sword* and *the Pentacle*. Later on, you will need a *Cauldron*, a *Wool Cloak*, a *Staff*, a *Knife*, a *Girdle*, and the *Magical Ring*. The last one is very special and often given as a gift, or a symbol of reaching a certain age, or for passing a certain kind of exam, called an Initiation.

I will explain all of them but for now you only need the four main tools. They are easy to make but you must make them as strong and as beautiful as you can. The more time you spend making them, the more magic they will hold. Remember this, your first tools will only hold as much magic as you can use safely; as you grow stronger and know more that will increase. *But* there will come a time when they can't hold any more because your magical power will have outgrown them. When that happens, you can do one of two things – you can wrap them in silk and put them away for a time when maybe, your own children will want to work magic and you can pass them on. *Or,* you can return each one to its original form. I will tell you how to do that later in the book.

The Wand

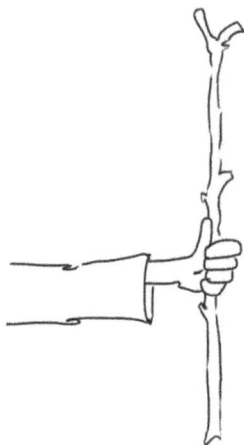

First on the list is the wand. Yes, I know you can buy one, especially if you've been to one of the Harry Potter theme parks, or a pagan fayre. But, when it comes to real magic, you need to personally make as many of the tools as you can. It takes longer, costs less, and will work better than anything you can buy. A wand needs to be strong, firm, not bendy and 'feel' right in your hand. It does *not* need to be strung with crystals, painted in colours, or have special handles of bone or metal. Your first tools need to be simple, useful, easy to carry round, and not the kind of thing that attracts attention.

Remember what I told you about not letting strangers know what you do or what you are. Showing any of your tools to friends, playmates, or, to use a Harry Potter word – *Muggles,* is a big no no!

A wand must be made of wood and not all woods make good wands. The best for this purpose come from hazel, hawthorn, rowan, oak, holly or blackthorn. Most woods can be used, but those are the most powerful. You need to visit the trees and spend time with them until one seems special. Sit with it, silent at first, then touch it, stroke it, talk to it, and bring a bottle of fresh water as a gift. Water from a running stream or river is the best of all gifts for a tree.

Explain to the tree that you would like to make a wand from one of its branches and ask if this is possible. Wait, listen and try to 'feel' the reply. It might be no. If that happens then thank the tree and look for another one. If you feel that the answer is yes, look for a branch that is suitable and within reach. Mark two to three inches from the trunk of the tree, and then measure the length you will need (not less than twelve and not more than sixteen inches is about right). It doesn't matter if the wood is not too straight, a slight twist or gnarl just makes it more personal. Too long and it is hard to carry around unseen, too little and it won't be strong enough to hold the power.

Tell the tree where you have marked it and ask it to prepare the branch for its removal. By choosing a few inches from the trunk it can grow a new branch. It will withdraw energy from that point but leave enough energy in the wood to act as a battery for the power you need. Doing this means you and the wand will share energy when it is used. Give the tree at least two weeks to prepare, and then cut the branch on a new moon with a very sharp knife. *(Ask an adult to do this so you don't cut yourself.)* Cut off the twigs and parts of the branch no longer needed and bury them under the roots of the tree with some water and a silver coin as an exchange.

Put the branch in a warm dry place like an airing cupboard or a shelf in the kitchen and let it dry out for two or three weeks. Then, you can either peel away the bark if you want to have the bare wood or leave the bark on for a natural look. I personally like to leave the bark on. If you peel it, then smooth the wood with a fine sandpaper and round off the two ends. You can now paint it with a clear varnish. Allow this to dry then add a second coat. Make sure both ends are trimmed and smooth. If you want, you can wrap one end with white cord for about three inches and glue the end, this gives a firm grip, or it can be left bare. As you work, talk to the wand explaining what you are doing, what it will be used for and how much you are looking forward to working with it.

Everything in this universe has a sense of *being*, to a greater or lesser extent, and if you talk to things and name them, that sense of *being* gets stronger. Many people give names to their cars, hoovers, washing machines and computers. We give names to our houses – it gives them a sense of being part of, and a share in, our life. So now is the time to name your wand. Nothing complicated but make sure it's not the name of a friend or one of the family, as that can make magical things go wrong at awkward moments. Maybe a favourite film or book character, or a name that explains something; Wind-Waver, Star-Bright, Shadow-Maker, Spell-Weaver, Red-Berry are all possibilities. But sometimes, the best names are short and simple, (my first wand was called Snoopy).

The Cup or Chalice

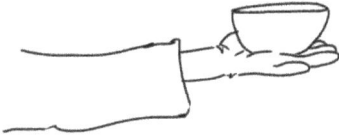

Next is the Cup or Chalice. Again, you have two choices, you can make one or you can buy or find one. Where magical tools are concerned remember this; they are not magical until they are *used* magically. *You* and the way *you* use them is what makes them magical. Strange as it may seem, you can take a mug out of the cupboard, use it magically, then wash it and put it back in the cupboard, again and again. The 'magic' will still work because of your *intent*. Adverts in magazines for 'magical equipment' are mostly a way for people to make money. They make wands and cups and so on because some people are too lazy to make their own, or because for some good reason they are unable to do so.

So, how do you make a cup? You can go to a craft shop and buy some clay and then use an old cup, a small bowl, or even an egg cup as a mould because your cup doesn't have to be big. Wet the clay, knead it until soft then carefully press the clay around the shape of the mould. (Rub the mould with oil first to make it easier to get the clay off afterwards and, if you are using an old cup, break the handle off first). The clay should be about half an inch thick maybe a little less. You might have to have two or three goes at this until you get it right. When you think it is the shape you want, let the clay harden for a while, then gently ease it off the mould and put it into the oven to bake really hard.

However, all this can take a long time, so there is another way. Look through the china in a thrift (or charity) shop and see if you can find an old cup with a nice shape. Take off the handle and file down the rough edges (ask an adult to do this for you.) If the weather is good leave the cup out in the sun for the whole day, moving it occasionally so it is in the sunlight all the time. If there is no sun, choose the night of a full moon and put the cup out in the moonlight. Both sun and moon light are good for cleansing things like this and they also fill it with their own power of light.

When your home-made cup is baked, you can paint it (use a paint that is free of anything poisonous) and line it with kitchen foil. It may not look very pretty, it may be a little shapeless, but you will have *made it with purpose* and that counts for a lot in magic. If you were given a christening cup when you were born, and if your parents agree, you can use that as your first magical cup; it will already hold the most magical thing of all – love.

The Sword

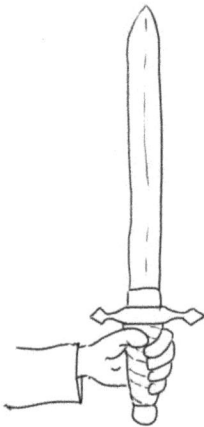

Now you have two of your tools, it is time for the sword.

We all know that swords can be dangerous things and, quite rightly, your parents won't let you have a real one until you are old enough to make your own decisions. Until then, you can use a "make believe" sword. I have already told you that believing in something is a magical act in itself. When you look at a caterpillar chewing on a leaf it doesn't seem possible that it can change into a butterfly, but the caterpillar *believes* it can and will, so it does, and it becomes something beautiful and different in every way from the caterpillar it once was. It is the same with magic – unless you believe in it, it can't happen. This is why you can make a sword out of cardboard and say to your magical inner self, 'this will be my sword' and it *will* be a sword for you, but for no one else.

You will need a piece of fairly strong cardboard that is about eighteen to twenty inches long, measuring tape, a felt pen, and something with a straight edge, to use as a guide. All you need is a basic sword shape such as the one pictured below. I would suggest you make two swords, so you have one in reserve.

(Why card and not wood.? Because wood can still cause serious injury if used wrongly. Cardboard will crumple on impact and is easily replaced).

Look at the pattern and note that it is very plain, its top edge should be *rounded not pointed*. When you are older you can look for a real sword and you will have a much wider choice, but my advice is, even then, to choose one with a blunted point, or have it rounded off by a blacksmith. Even the best magicians have had accidents with sharp swords.

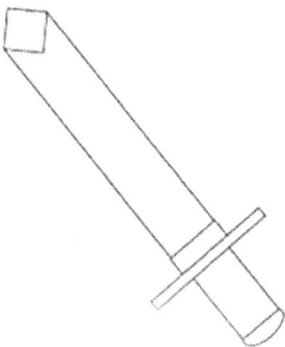

Using the picture as a pattern, measure off between eighteen to twenty inches for the blade, *not* the hilt, and outline the shape with the felt pen. It is best to use a sharp craft knife to cut the shape out of the card, rather than using scissors. Again, *ask an adult* to do this for you. You don't want to get blood on your sword – just yet! Now for the hilt. For this you will need to cut out two shapes in the same way as the blade. Why two? Because the hilt needs to be stronger than the blade, so the pieces will be glued together with the lower part of the sword held between them. This will give you something firm to hold and it won't split easily if roughly handled. Now cover the blade with silver foil – do this carefully and try to make it as smooth as you can. Cover the two hilt pieces with strong glue and slide at least two inches of the 'blade' between them. Then place a weight, such as a heavy book, on the hilt to hold it in place until the glue sets. Cover the hilt with silver foil like the blade, or you can paint it.

You now have a sword that can be used safely (although still with care). It will be as magical as a real weapon, but much safer. You should still take care when using it; never wave it near your face or anyone else's.

One last thing about magical swords; they all have names. In fact they often have three of them. The first is the name given them by the blacksmith who made them, the second is the name their new owner gives them, and the third is the name the sword calls itself. This is the strongest name of all, and it can take many years of use before the sword feels the bond between it and its owner is strong enough for that name to be shared. Think long and hard about the name you give your sword; it is very important. It may take several tries before the sword accepts the name you choose so take your time and ask the sword to help you. It may only be a make-believe sword, but its spirit is that of a real sword and, if you treat it with respect, it will look after you until the time when its work is done.

The Pentacle

Now there is just the pentacle (sometimes called a pantacle) to make and this is the easiest of all. In ancient times this was usually made from a circle of wood cut from a tree trunk, the five-pointed star was carved into it

and the whole thing was polished. This method is still used today. However, you can make one from a coloured paper plate, or, as you did with the cup,

look in a thrift shop for an old plate with enough plain space in the middle to paint the five-pointed star. If you use a paper plate use two or three together to give it weight and substance. Paste them firmly and allow to dry overnight, then very carefully trace the five-pointed star in the centre. This is a very ancient symbol and brings together the *five* elements used in magic. Yes, *five*.

* The first downward stroke represents *earth*.
* The second is angled up and to the side and represents *water*.
* The third is across the middle and stands for *fire*.
* Down again at an angle represents *air*.
* Finally, up to join with the first line which represents *spirit*.

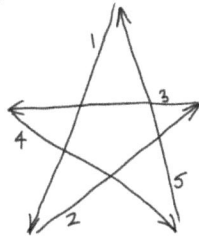

Practice drawing this a few times, then do it in pencil on the plate before going over it in felt tip and letting it dry. If you like, you can then decorate the plate with stick-on symbols to represent earth; flowers, trees, animals or whatever else you like.

Cover the symbols with transparent tape to keep them fresh and clean. You can also put the same kind of tape around the edges of the plate to keep it all together. If you use a real plate, make sure there is enough space to paint the five-pointed star. You now have your four magical tools.

Do you want to know a secret?

You can make magic using a wooden pencil for a wand, (it's made of wood), a coconut shell or even an acorn cup as a chalice, (it will hold water), a big darning needle for a sword, (it has a sharp point), and a large leaf as a pentacle (use it to hold the bread offering). It's not the tools that are magic, it is *you* and *your* intention that makes it work. Magic comes from within the person, not from the tools: they are just symbols of the magic already inside the person.

In the next chapter I'll tell you about the other things you will need later on, and also about the special ceremony you will have to make them ready to use. I will also tell you how to 'send them back' when their work is done, and you no longer need to use them.

Chapter Four
Magical Tools and How to Make Them
(Part Two)

I always believe in looking ahead, so I know what is coming, which is why I am going to tell you about some of the other tools you may need as you get older. Some of these are not always used as much as in times long past, but you can never know 'too much', and the more you know about the history of paganism, the more you will understand how and why you are different to other people.

You will certainly have seen pictures of a witch and her cauldron in fairy tale books, and a cauldron is one of the tools you may need in the future. In ancient times, it was an everyday household article that was hung over a fire for cooking and for heating water. Gradually, it became linked to the ordinary person's idea of witchcraft. The truth is that it was never exclusively used in magic. Meals were cooked in it and so were the herbal brews that were the only medicines available at that time. Today witches often use a cauldron to cook food, or as a container for fresh food to hand around after a woodland ritual. You can still buy them in specialist shops, and even in some garden centres, where they are used as garden ornaments or as plant pots. As you grow in knowledge, you might like to study herbal lore, in which case a cauldron will be useful.

The Staff

A staff – again this was something in everyday use once upon a time. In the films of *The Hobbit* and *The Lord of the Rings*, you may have seen Gandalf, the wizard, using a staff instead of a wand. More often it was used as a support because people walked everywhere, and it was something strong to lean on when you were tired. Like the cauldron, they had two uses; one magical and one for everyday.

Magical staffs are often used in ritual by the person leading the ceremony or, in some groups, as a symbol of a special authority. In England especially this was so and those who made them were known as Cudgel Masters. Now there is really only one such person left. Here is a picture of a Cudgel Master.

The Magical Knife

A magical knife is also something you will need later. At the moment though, sharp knives are not something you will be using – too many accidents can happen with them. But you can read about them and get to know how to use them. There are two different kinds – the athame, (pronounced *a-thay-mee*), which has a black handle, usually horn or carved wood that has been dyed black. This is often worn in a leather sheath and hung on the girdle (belt). It is used to draw symbolic signs in the air and to cut cords and bindings. The boline (pronounced *boll-een*) is a white-handled knife, again usually made of horn. The blade is curved like the crescent moon and is rather like a sickle, only smaller. The boline is used to cut corn sheaves in harvest festivals. Such knives have many uses which you will come to know as you get older.

The Cord

A cord may be worn around the waist of your robe like a belt. Different groups use different colours to symbolise the rank of a group member. For instance, a newcomer might wear a white cord, then after a while will be allowed to change it for a green one, and then for maybe a blue or red one. Colours depend on the rules of the group. There are, as a general rule, three levels or *degrees*. A person beginning their first degree might be known as a neophyte, newcomer or Initiate of the First Degree. Then there is a second and often a third degree, each of which would have their own colour associated with them. As you are very new to magic, you should use a plain white cord (a dressing gown cord is ideal for this as it often has tassels on each end.)

Incense

Later on, when you are older, you can add an incense burner to your tools but, as this also means using matches and having burning charcoal or incense sticks around, you must wait until your parents think that you are old enough. Even then, always make sure you have water close by in case of accidents. Incense is not important at this time though, and you can work without it.

The Cloak

A wool cloak is very useful in cold weather, when you are working magic outside. Cloaks are cut very full to wrap around you. They should come down to the ankle and, if they are not made of wool, they should be made of fairly thick cloth or felt and lined to give protection from the weather. They should also have a hood lined with something warm.

The Robe

A robe is something you will need quite soon. They are easy to make, or you can buy them. Robes are simple and should be made of a material that can be washed often. Long sleeves, but not too full as this can knock things over and, if too near to a candle, might just catch fire. Many people have a light cotton one for summer and a thicker one for winter. The hood gives privacy when you are meditating or just being quiet. You will sometimes hear or read about witches wearing nothing at all in their ceremonies. Well, that might be alright if you live in a very warm climate. But it is nicer to be warm and it's a lot less embarrassing for you and everyone else if you wear a robe. The traditional witches' hat you can buy at Halloween at any super market. *But*, although they have come to be seen as part of a traditional witches' outfit, in fact they have no real power and you don't need one. In Wales, in the United Kingdom, such a hat is part of the national costume and they are still worn at festivals.

The Ring

The ring is a very important piece of magical jewellery. It really needs to be made specially for you and should fit the first finger of your right hand. Some groups like everyone to have the same stone, as it brings the group closer together – other groups allow you to choose your own stone. Its design can be anything you choose. *However, you do not need such a ring yet... you must first prove you are worthy to have one, through your work, your studies and your determination to learn as much as you can.*

Caring for Your Tools

All tools should be kept separate from other everyday things like clothes, toys, books etc. Keep them in a special box or drawer and wrap each one in a piece of clean cotton. The smaller things can be covered with a clean handkerchief, and the larger ones in a pillow case. When you are older and have gathered the tools you will use from then on, they should be wrapped in silk, but for now cotton is good.

Never use your magical tools for anything but magical work, unless it is an emergency. If you need tools and you are not at home, look around you and see what can be used on the spur of the moment. A piece of wood can become a wand, a thorn or sharp stone can be used as a sword, a flower head makes a cup and a leaf, piece of paper, or bark from a tree can be a pentacle. I tell my students that they can work magic in a desert, with nothing but sand around, because your left forefinger can be a wand, the right forefinger can be a sword, your two hands together become a cup and one hand is the pentacle. You are never without magical tools if you remember this.

Dolores Ashcroft-Nowicki

Consecrating Your Tools

What makes tools special? Your belief in them is all you need in an emergency, but real ones need to be 'blessed' or consecrated before you use them for the first time.

Consecration is a big word but a very important one. It can have many different meanings but the one you need to know about simply means: *'To make something special, or Holy.'*

For the consecration, you'll need a clean cloth, a small table, fresh water, a candle, a saucer of oil, and some salt. Lay the clean cloth on the table and arrange your tools in a line. Make sure your hands are clean and, if possible, wear your new robe. If you don't have one yet, just clean clothes will do. Keep remembering that 'magic' comes from within *you*. Tools and robes are extras to help you concentrate. Ask an adult to light the candle if you are not allowed to do so yourself.

Stand at the table for a few moments and think about what you are going to do. You are going to bless the tools you have made and make them special.

The Blessing Ceremony

Each of the four major tools holds the power of an element (earth, water, fire, and air) and has a dedicated direction. Some witches say the wand holds the power of fire; others say it is the power of air. I personally use it as a power of air because its direction is to the east, the direction of air, and it directs things like a signpost.

First you need to bless the salt, water, candle and oil. Hold your right hand over the water and say:

Creature of the great oceans, I bless you in the name of the Great Being that created you.

Now pour half a teaspoon of salt into your left hand, hold your right hand over it and say:

Creature of earth, I bless you in the name of the Great Being that created you.

Then pour the salt into the water.

Next, take the lighted candle (make sure you have permission from your parents, and it would be a good idea to have at least one of them with you). Hold it up high and say:

Creature of fire, I bless you in the name of the Great Being that created you.

Now, take the feather, dip the tip in the oil and say:

Creature of air, I bless you in the name of the Great Being that created you.

Take the wand in your right hand and hold it up as high as you can. Holding something up to the light is an ancient way of offering something to the sun, which has always been seen as a symbol of something good to believe in. As you hold it up, think of it as being covered with tiny lights, which sink into it and make it glow. Then lay it down in front of you, sprinkle it with salt and water and say:

With the spirit of salt and water, I bless and consecrate this wand that it may help me in my magical work, and I name it..................

Next, pass the wand through the candle flame (make sure you do not touch the flame with your hands or your sleeve) and say:

By the spirit of flame, I bless and consecrate this wand to my service that it may direct my will in a true and proper manner according to the laws of Magic and I name it ....

Finally dip the feather into the oil and stroke the wand with it from top and to bottom and say:

By the spirit of this symbol of air touched by blessed oil, I bless and consecrate this wand that it may serve me with honour. When it is time, I vow to return this wand to the place of its beginning that it may bring a blessing to all of its kind. I name this wand.................

Your wand is now ready to use. Wrap it in a clean cloth and put it aside.

The next tool is your sword. Place it on the table. The salt and water, candle and oil are already blessed, so you don't have to do that again.

Take the sword in your right hand and hold it up high as you can. As you hold it up, think of it as being made of silver and glowing with magical power. Then lay it down in front of you and sprinkle it with salt and water and say:

With the spirit of salt and water, I bless and consecrate this sword that it may protect me and my magical work and help me to protect and help others in need. I name this sword.................

Now pass it through the candle flame (very carefully for remember this sword is made of cardboard and can catch fire easily) and say:

By the spirit of flame, I bless and consecrate this sword. May it give me the courage to do what is right and to keep faith with the ancient laws of magic. I name it ....

Now dip the feather into the oil and stroke the blade of the sword with it and say:

By the spirit of this symbol of air, touched by blessed oil, I bless and consecrate this Sword that it may serve me and those I need to protect. May it never be used in anger or without due care and attention to the laws of magic. When it is time, I vow to bury this sword in a place suitable for something sacred, that it may return to the earth. I name this Sword..................

Wrap the sword in a clean cloth and put it aside.

Now take the cup in both hands. Lift it high and imagine it filled with liquid light, so full that it spills over and flows into your hands. Lay it down on the table and say:

By the spirit of salt and water, I bless and consecrate this cup that it may fill me and my magical work with strength and love for all life. May it make me able to be the best I can be. All sacred cups have the same name... that name is Love.

Now pass it through the candle flame (again carefully) and say:

By the spirit of flame, I bless and consecrate this cup. May it fill me with knowledge, understanding and compassion. As a symbol of the Cup of Cups, may it fill me with the light and love that is the wine within it. I pronounce its name and that name is Love.

Now dip the feather into the oil, run it around the outside of the cup and say:

By the spirit of this symbol of air, touched by blessed oil, I bless and consecrate this cup that it may help me to work magic in a way that causes no harm. When it is time, I will break it into pieces so no unclean hands may touch it. I will bury it in a place of beauty suitable for something sacred, that it may return to the earth. The name of this cup is Love.

Wrap the cup in a cloth and put it away safely.

Now take the pentacle in your hands and hold it up. Imagine it carrying a piece of bread covered with honey. Then place a small piece of bread on it and put both on the table. Sprinkle it with salt and water and say:

By the spirit of salt and water, I bless and consecrate this pentacle and the bread it carries that it may fill me with the strength to do what is good and right. Its magical name will be..................

Now pass it through the candle flame (carefully) and say:

By the spirit of flame, I bless and consecrate this pentacle. May the bread it carries fill me with gentleness, helpfulness and love towards all life forms, and the desire to help others. Its name is..................

Now dip the feather into the oil and run it around the outer rim of the pentacle and say:

By the spirit of this symbol of air, touched by blessed oil, I bless and consecrate this pentacle that it may help me to understand the true meaning of giving. To receive one must first give. The offering of bread to those in need is an ancient blessing, for those who offer without thinking of themselves will receive in kind. When it is time, I will return it to the earth where it will bless the ground around it. The name of this pentacle is..................

Again, wrap it up carefully and put it away.

Keep these magical tools safe and away from prying eyes. They are not to be passed around to friends but kept only for your magical work. The fewer who know that you have them, the more powerful their work will be.

The ritual of blessing your magical tools is very important. It is not a game in the way you play a game on a computer. It is a very serious promise made in a sacred way, in a sacred place. You are old enough to understand what is right and what is wrong. You are also old enough to understand this:

Everything in this world is connected simply by being alive. A tree, an animal, a fish or bird, the flowers in your garden, the fruit in an orchard, the earth you walk on; all this is alive. Sometimes it is hard to understand this because of the different forms life can take. The chair you sit on is made of wood, and the wood remembers once being part of a tree. Even plastic is made of something that has a kind of life. You are connected to everything and everything is connected to you.

Not many people think like this, but you are special, and you can begin to see everything around you as something you can communicate with in different ways. Witches *live in the world,* but they also feel themselves to be part of everything around them. In the same way that a cat or dog can understand most of what you say to them through the sound of your voice or the way you touch them, so a tree or a garden and even things like mountains, rivers and lakes can understand how you feel when you are with them and have ways in which they can let you know they understand. Stand in a garden in the evening after sunset and you can feel the life around you settling down for the night. Listen to the wind moving through a cornfield just before harvest and it is like listening to a song. Just being alive and knowing it is an adventure. Try to make each day special: learn a new word, write out a wish 100 times and bury it under tree. Look around you and try to see something you never noticed before. Write a spell or a wish, tie it to the branch of a tree and let the air elementals give it power to come true. In Ireland, many people especially those living in the country, often do this. They leave prayers, messages to those who have passed on or just wishes for something special. In chapter six I will tell you all about making spells – it is not as easy as you might think – but I will also share some very old spells with you.

There is a ritual I was taught when I was young, and I would like to pass it on to you. My grandmother told me that the moon had special powers, especially when she was new. When I saw the new moon for the first time each month, I was to bow to her three times three (nine times), cross the fingers of my right hand and say:

Lady Moon, Lady Moon,
Walking in your silver shoon (shoes).
Blessed Be your shining light.
Blessed Be my sleep this night.

Then I was to make a wish and, if the moon was in a good mood, she might grant it. Sometimes she did and sometimes she didn't. But I still make nine bows to her when I see the new moon.

Remember: The way of magic is the way of adventure.

Chapter Five
Familiars and Invisible Friends

This is a long chapter, because it needs a lot of explaining. You may have read about familiars in stories about witches. So what is a familiar? Well, witches believe there are other kinds of beings living in this world besides us. A lot of them can't be seen, because their bodies are much finer than ours and this makes them invisible to us. but there are a few who *can* see them, especially children, but they look so ordinary you don't always know they're not really there. When you start school, you are so busy learning things like grammar and maths, and history that you forget to see the '*invisible*' world about you. If you are part of a pagan family, you will be encouraged to keep 'seeing' things like this.

Some children have friends that others can't see. Often these friends are not like us at all. They might have small wings, tails, or even tiny horns. They may have animal shapes and be quite big, but often they are small and can be naughty at times and they like to play tricks. Many grown-up witches have friends like this who become friends and protectors and we use the word *familiar* to describe them.

Long ago, when it was dangerous to be a witch, many of the older ones were lonely and often lived away from other people. Ordinary people were afraid of them and didn't talk to them. So many witches had small animals as friends instead. Mostly they were real ones, but some had friends which took the form of animals that ordinary people could not see. Sometimes they had two or three different ones. Usually they were cats or dogs or maybe a bird, like owls, rooks, magpies, and crows.

Not all witches had real pets. Some of them, the really clever ones, learned to make friends with the *elementals;* wood sprites and the little beings that were, and are, the energy forms of plants. Because they didn't want people to know they were witches, they asked their invisible friends to make themselves forms that looked like everyday pets.

Sometimes, these friends are strong enough to create bodies that can be seen by everyone. But it's hard to keep them visible for long and it uses a lot of energy. How do they become real? Are they dangerous? (And no – you can't buy them from a pet shop.)

What are they? We don't really know, but many pagan people think there are beings in another dimension that are full of energy but can only live in our dimension if they can find a form to live in or can share a form already inhabited. What we *think* happens is that they might ask a small life form like a cat, a dog, a bird, or maybe a toad n a pond if they can share its form. In return, they give the animal a longer life, and more intelligence than they would have normally. Some animals have intelligence far beyond what would be normal for them. Then they can be a real companion to the witch and keep her from being lonely.

Another explanation might be that they are an elemental energy, (Earth=gnome, Water=mermaid or nixie, Fire=salamander, and Air=sylph/fairy) that is attracted to someone with similar energy – especially a young person – and use their energy for a short time to become 'real'. These energy beings often have powers that seem magical to us. But they try not to use too much human energy as it can make you very tired, This is the reason why some elemental familiars often disappear for a while, so they don't use too much of your energy.

Are they harmful to us? No, but they need our human energy to become *real*. *They understand this* and also that when children begin school, their attention and energy need to go into schoolwork, new friends and games. There's not so much energy available, and the link with the familiar often ends until the human person grows up and understands more about the use of energy.

So, a familiar is an energy form that can link with a human being of any age, who has energy to spare or an animal form, in order to become visible for short periods of time. In return for the gift of energy, which for them is like a visit to Disneyland, they often share their powers *for a while*. This is why children like you often see things grown-ups can't see.

But a few people attract a different kind of energy, and

they keep that energy by them all through their lives. I had two such energy friends when I was young. The first was a girl like me and I called her Dodo. She stayed with me until I went to school, but years later, when my cousin was born, Dodo returned and became her friend until she went to school. When my cousin grew up, she had a daughter of her own who one day came in and asked her mother for an extra biscuit for her 'friend' Dodo! So a familiar can be passed from one generation to another.

I had another familiar friend, who lived in a very old granite wall that I passed on my way to school every day. He was an earth elemental and I called him Christopher. I used to stop and talk to him on my way to and from school. He was with me for almost a year, then a teacher caught me 'talking to a wall', and after that Christopher left and never returned.

Familiars can appear without warning, often when you are quite young. There are stories that tell of small children and babies acting as if they are playing with someone and talking to them. Also, old tales of 'changelings' when, supposedly, the fairies would take the real child and leave a strange fairy child in its place. A true familiar is always friendly, and often acts as a protector, so enjoy their company while you can.

It is possible to actually make *a different kind of familiar* called a *thoughtform*, and if you build it carefully it can attract an elemental or nature spirit for a while. But that is a very grown up way to do it, and you have other things to do and see before then. When you grow up, and if you have the right kind of psychic power, you may be able to work with a spiritual teacher who, though not seen, can train you in the old ways of magic. But that is for a different kind of book.

So, adding all this together what do we have?

Having a familiar is serious magic and not to be used without care until you know a lot more about magic. You need to think about why you want this kind of friend. Maybe you have no brothers or sisters, or don't make friends easily. You might be bullied at school and made to feel unwanted. The important thing about familiars is *secrecy*. Of course, your parents will know. They will notice the difference in you. But it is not something for others to know. At best, you will be made fun of, at worse it could interfere with your school work. If you boast about it, it will disappear and may take a long time before any familiar will trust you again.

Thoughtform friends are like day-dreams but stronger, and making one needs patience. With a note-pad and a pen, write down why you want to make one. 'Just for fun' is not a good answer. This kind of magic is not used for *fun*, but to help you understand there are many kinds of life forms. Some are kind and helpful, and some are not. So you must be clear about *why* you want such a friend.

If you have pagan parents or older friends, you can go to them for advice. Thoughtforms can just be companions, who are there to make life easier, or you can have adventures with them, or they can be mischievous; it depends on the kind of form you make. A thoughtform takes time to make in the right way. First, you must understand *that it really is made of your thoughts*. Read this carefully for it is the basis of all real magic, not the Disney world kind. Everything in your house, from the bed you sleep in, to the clothes you wear, the saucepan in the kitchen and the carpet on the floor, has become real because of thought. Somebody *thought* up a shape for your bed, designed the chairs, the saucepans and the

Dolores Ashcroft-Nowicki

pattern on the carpet. Before that, they were just *ideas* and ideas are little thoughtforms. You have to think about how you want your familiar to look. Remember, this will only to be seen by *you* – it will not be 'real' to anyone else. Decide if it will be an animal, a fairy, or an elemental, which can mean a gnome, undine, sylph or a salamander.

A gnome is an earth elemental and they are usually quite small. They have beards (even the lady gnomes) and they wear sturdy hard-wearing clothes, nearly always with a scarlet jacket or hat and leather boots. They work hard in the earth, tending to the roots of growing things. They are also very busy, so they don't have a lot of time to spare. However, they are kind and friendly, unless you do something to hurt the earth, then they can get angry.

Sylphs are air elementals and rather like fairies; almost transparent and you can see through them. They are rather dreamy and often disappear when the wind blows because they love to dance with the wind.

Undines (the proper word for mermaids) do not make good familiars because they need to be in water and water is dangerous for human beings. They don't understand that and want to get you into the water to play. So don't choose an undine.

Nor are salamanders a good choice because they are fire elementals and, until you are older and have more experience, they can also be dangerous. Salamanders are usually seen to be rather like fiery lizards. If you look at flames in a fire, you can see they change shape and wriggle around a lot like lizards. So think of a snakelike tongue of flame as a basic form.

All in all, gnomes are your best choice. They are small, friendly, good-natured and protective. Also, they are willing to take animal form sometimes as they are fond of them. However, as they work with the earth, they may not always be there to talk to you.

You can *think up* a form of your own. Big dogs are good thoughtforms. They don't need feeding because they live off energy and they don't need to go on long walks. Cats make good thoughtforms, especially black ones, and all cats are naturally magical. The good thing about thoughtforms is that they can grow big if they need to protect you, and they can be set to guard you against bad dreams when you sleep, but they can also be very small, small enough to hide in tiny places. It can be anything from a lion to a frog or toad – all of which are magical creatures and found in fairy tales. Or you can '*thoughtform*' a fairy creature. Your familiar really can be anything you want it to be.

Find a picture of the animal or gnome you want and keep it with you. Make several copies and put one under your pillow and a small one in your pocket or school bag. If anyone asks you why you have you have it, you can say truthfully that you like the picture or that kind of animal. Whenever you have a few minutes alone, sit quietly and try to imagine the animal or gnome is sitting in front of you. Try to '*see*' it inside your head. Think of the animal's fur and how soft and silky it feels when you stroke it. Listen to the cat's purr or hear the black dog bark. See the big grin on the face of the gnome and the red jacket they always wear. If you are good at art, draw a picture of them. *But keep making their picture inside your head.*

When you have the picture really clear, begin to think of a name for your familiar. Make it short and easy to remember. Listen to the sound of the name in your head until you can hear it clearly. *Remember what I told you about magical names and how important they are.*

Now comes the hard part: when you dream, there is a part of you that enters what we might call a *dream world,* (some call it the *astral world.*) There are many kinds of worlds – the one you live in, often called the *real* world, which is where you are now. Then there is the *dream world,* which is not like this one at all. Think of it as being filled with a white misty fog. This mist can take any form you like; a building, an animal, an ocean, a wood, anything at all. Then there is the *mental* or *mind world* and above that what we might think of as being the *angelic world.*

But we are concerned with the *dream world.* Find a quiet place where you will be undisturbed, close your eyes and stay still for a few minutes. Then inside your head, as if in a dream clear a space around you and imagine being in a garden – your own or one you know. Make pictures in your head about what you see – grass, flowers, bushes, trees. As you think about them, they take shape, until you can feel you are in a garden filled with plants and flowers. You need it to keep that shape even when you are not there. So imagine a wooden seat somewhere in this dream garden, with your name on it in gold letters. Any time you want to be in the garden just close your eyes, take a deep breath and see that wooden seat with your name on it, and it will build up around you. It may take an effort at first, but as you do it more and more it will be easier.

You might like to imagine the garden surrounded by a wall with a gate, again with a sign on it saying your name. You can even imagine a key for the gate. All you need to do to be in the garden is imagine yourself in front of the gate and you will be there.

It is best to do this when you are alone and in a safe place. Not with a lot of people around you. This is your secret place, where you can come to talk and play with your familiar, or somewhere to come if you feel the need to be alone. You can add a summer house, or a pond with gold fish. It is a *safe* place where you can go if you are sad, lonely, afraid, or upset. Then you can sit in your secret garden and talk to your familiar friend or to the gnomes who work in the garden.

To do this, pull into the garden some of the white misty stuff this world is made from. Think about how you want to see him or her. Imagine the clothes, the heavy boots, the scarlet jacket and hat. A girl gnome will have an apron as well. You can make them your own age or older. Older is nice as they can teach you more. Make your mind-picture as real as you can, then touch your head with your first finger and say:

Being of earth, now come to me.
Accept the place I've made for thee.
I offer my hand so we may be,
Friends together, just you and me.
Here in this place, we can meet and play,
Be it night or be it day.
In this world we can play a game,
Human and element both the same.
A name I offer to be your own,
A garden I offer to be your home.
Being of earth now let us be,
Friends together you and me.

Call out the name you have chosen to give your gnome and wait. It may take several times before there is an answer as gnomes are shy of humans. Remember they may not be visible until they get to know you. They will find a place in the garden where they can work with the earth but can come if you call them. Always bless them before leaving and say: *'Be Blessed for your work.'*

Sometimes people move from one country to another. In the last century, many people left Europe and moved to America. When this happens local elementals and spirits often move with them. So they have to make friends with the spirits of the new land. This is not easy, as every land has its own spirits and elementals and it takes time to work together. Ask your parents to find you a film called *Finian's Rainbow*. It shows you how difficult it is for the *'little people'* to mix with those in the new land. You can call on the elementals of the new land you have moved to, but if you have ancestors who came from Europe it might be easier to call a familiar from the Old Country.

This is *small* magic. Deep magic comes later, when you are older. Until then, be content with a familiar companion. In the next chapter we will talk about spells, chants, and songs you can learn and use.

Chapter Six

Spells, Chants and Dances

Since the earliest times we humans have danced to express our feelings both of joy and sorrow. Then we learned to use language and used it to express thoughts and ideas in words. Over thousands of years we have used both in our lives, in ways of tradition, religions and as art forms. When it comes to magic, they are both very important. So, let's take spells first.

First, what is a spell? It's a string of words put together in a special way that contains a wish, a hope, a request, a blessing or a curse, and no I am not going to tell you how to do curses, as I want you to uphold the witches' rule. Remember? *And it harm none.*

Secondly, to work properly and be effective, a spell must have four parts; it must rhyme, it must have rhythm, it must be aimed, and it must have emotion behind it. Without those four things it won't work, or it won't work with any great effect, which after all is what it is supposed to do.

Thirdly, you don't put a spell *on* people or animals unless it's a healing or protective spell, and they are different to other spells. To do so violates the Witches' Rule.

You make a spell to cause an effect. When you are older, you might come across books of spells that *do* act on people, but that is the reason a lot of people think badly of witches.

Spells must rhyme – why? Firstly, because it makes them easier to remember. Secondly, rhyme stirs up emotion, and without emotion no spell will work, and finally rhyme gives extra power to the rhythm.

Here are some examples of spells that are hundreds of years old:

To Heal Cuts and Bruises (1775)

By love and will and herb I heal
This unkind cut I seek to seal
From pain and bleeding now be free
And as I say so mote it be.

Circle Casting Spell (1) (1793)

Magic in and magic out,
Magic all around about.
Within this circle safe are we,
As I will so mote it be.

Circle Casting Spell (2) (1810)

By hill and moon and Lady bright
And by the rowan tree,
Now I cast my spell this night
And call my power to me.

Circle Spell (3) (1815)

Within this circle cast by me,
I circle others, bound are we.
With salt and herb and whispered charm
I do my will but cause no harm.
As midnight calls the witching hour,
At quarters four I raise my power.
Earth and Water, Fire and Air
This I do and this I dare.
So, before the power be spent,
I now declare my full intent.

To Make a Wish Come True

By horn and hoof and silver moon,
I summon power to grant a boon.
I wish I may, I wish I might
Be granted grace this very night.

The following spells were written by girls in the 1700s:

To Cast Away Trouble – Loveday Malpas, aged 14, 1716

By my will and by my power,
Summon I within this hour,
Let this trouble pass from me,
And as I will so mote it be.

To Raise the Wind – Prudence Ostler, aged 14, 1716

I summon up and summon in
The elements to please my whim.

Dolores Ashcroft-Nowicki

Spirits rise and be as one.
Do as I will, and it harm none.

When *spoken* aloud, these lines have both rhyme and rhythm and, if repeated in the traditional three times three, they begin to vibrate and send the spell outwards.

The best spells are those you make yourself, and there are ways to make it easier. You just need to know a traditional beginning and ending and then make up the bit in between. Here are a few beginnings you can use.

Beginning lines

By my will and by my power.
I summon up and summon in
On this day and in this hour.
Fairy Folk and Fairy Kin

Or:

By will of wand and strength of sword,
By witch's power and witch's word,
By hoof and horn and rowan tree.
Now I call my power to Me.

Or:

By the moon upon the hill
By witch's power and witch's will.

You can then add another two lines containing your actual spell and end it with a traditional ending such as:

Now all is said, the spell is run,
I turn three times and it is done.

Or:

Now by all the spirits bright,
I send this spell by witch's might.

Or:

I spin three times and bend the knee,
And as I will so mote it be.

Spell casting can be hard at first but, as you find more
words that rhyme, it will get easier. Below you will find
some old spells that will show you how to put them
together. As long your spell rhymes, you can bend the
rules. Below are some examples.

By Air and Water, Fire and Earth,
By love that brings all things to birth,

(This is the start of spell, now add your intent. For
example,)

Tomorrow's test I need to win.
I summon up and summon in,
Witch and warlock, faerie kind,
Unlock the answers in my mind.

(And to end the spell, for example)

Share your power to do my will,
To work for good and not for ill.

Or perhaps:

By hill and moon and Lady bright
And by the rowan tree,
By witch's skill and witch's might
I weave and chant my spell this night.
Tomorrow's test I need to pass,
That in the class I be not last.
I spin three times and bow the knee
And as I will so mote it be.

Rhyming is very important in weaving spells, but you can
buy a book called *The Poet's Manual and Rhyming*

Dictionary that will be very useful.

What kind is spell is right for you? Friendship spells, healing spells, protection spells (including protecting against nightmares) are some of the most common spells that you may want to perform.

Friendship Spell

The thing about friends is that they can change, move away, or stop being friendly for many different reasons. This makes it difficult to weave a friendship spell, so accept that some things can only last for a certain time. You need two cords (dressing gown cords or ribbons will do.) One should be gold and the other silver (or white.) Bless them as you have blessed your tools and write your magical name on one and the friend's name on the other. Then, as you speak the spell, knot them together four times. Cut between the two halves and give one piece to your friend and keep the other one. The knots must *not* be undone, or the friendship will not last.

Important: The other person must know what you want to do and agree to it. Don't do this spell unless you both agree. To break the spell, wash your cord in running water, bless it and bury it in the garden then sow some seeds over it. This will keep what is left of the friendship growing but let the rest go without regret.

The Spell

I call upon the angels bright,
To help me weave a spell this night,
With cords of silver and of gold,
I fashion what cannot be sold.
Friendship links us hand to hand,
Together we will make our stand.

But if one day that link should break,
I'll wish you well, tho' hearts will ache.
But as of now together we,
Will stand tho' what will be, will be.

Dream Troll Spell

Now for something a little different.

A troll is not always 'nasty' or a scary creature that lives under a bridge. Dream trolls are helpful.

If you are troubled with bad dreams, try making a *Dream Troll*. Look for a small figure of something strong for a dream guardian. The figure should be small enough to go under your pillow. It can be a knight in armour, but animals are best; a horse, bull, lion, dog, tiger, or dragon would all work well. You can find inexpensive miniatures in toy shops. The intent behind a dream troll is that it goes into your dreams with you and guards you against anything that might scare you. It may be small during the day, but at night it grows as large as it needs to be to protect you. It is like a familiar but is made for only one purpose – to keep you safe in your dreams. A familiar's form is made from your imagination, while a dream troll is an actual figure in the day time but comes to life in your dreams. You may not always see it when you dream, but if something frightens you it will protect you. It can change size and shape to deal with whatever is there.

Once you have your guardian token, you need to choose a name for it and then wash it (even if it's newly-bought other people will have touched it.) As you do so, repeat the name you have chosen for it. Remember how you blessed the salt and water when you made your tools? Make some more and then put the miniature in it and leave it overnight, then dry it with a clean cloth. Now sit in a quiet place with the figure held between your hands. Hold its name in your mind and think about being quiet inside yourself. Begin to think of each breath you take being full of starlight, lighting you up from the inside like a Christmas tree. When you breathe out, breathe the light over and into the Guardian. Do this three times, then pause and breathe normally. Repeat the breathing process twice more, making three times three in all.

Now for the spell.

On a small table put a clean white cloth – a serviette, tissue, or handkerchief will do. Put the image on it and sprinkle a circle of salt around it. This keeps away anything that might work against your spell. Stand up straight, holding your wand, and make sure you feel quiet inside, then walk around the table three times clockwise. Face the east, hold out the wand and say:

On this day and in this hour,
I summon by my inner power.
An angel bright with wings outspread,
to guard my room and bless my bed. (turn to the South)
I now reach out to the Fair Folk all
to come to me if I should call. (turn to the West)
A Dream Troll now will guard my sleep
And nightmares all their distance keep. (turn to North)
Dream Troll now awake and be
My night time guardian three times three.

Put the image under the mattress cover of your bed where it will be safe. Before you sleep, reach out and touch it and say its name, then it will wake up and do guard duty all night. When you are older and no longer need it, you can pass it to a younger person by giving them its name.

Spells have a lot in common with nursery rhymes and playground games. Both have rhythms, rhyme and often actions to go with them, and most have a hidden meaning or origin. Such as:

Ring-a Ring-a Rosies
A pocket full of posies
Atishoo Atishoo,
We all fall down

This rhyme relates to the Black Death, or Plague, that killed thousands of people in the Middle Ages. The Ring of Rosies refers to the red rash of the infection on the body. The Pocket full of Posies is the pomander or bunch of herbs used to keep away the smell of the sickness. Sneezing was held to be the first sign of the infection after which the victim 'fell down' dead. Here's another example:

Baa baa black sheep have you any wool?
Yes sir, yes sir, three bags full!
One for the master, one for the dame
But none for the little boy who cries down the lane.
(Final line until the late sixteenth century)

In the fifteenth and sixteenth century, wool was an important part of Britain's economy and everyone wanted a part of it. A farmer might have enough sheep to produce just two or three bags of wool. One bag was taken by the Lord of the Manor for whom the farmer worked the land. One bag was taken by the Church (the Dame) and half of the last bag would be taken in lieu of taxes, hence there would be little or none left for 'the little boy' (the farmer) who lives down the lane. There are books that explain the old meaning of these rhymes but not all of them are suitable for this book

Chants

Chants are different to spells, more like hymns in church, but rhyming is still an important part of them. They are mainly used when working in a circle with a group but can be used by one person. There are books you can buy with collections of chants, but not all will be suitable. In magic, it is always best to make your own rituals, spells and chants. Even if they don't sound as good as the ones in a book, the fact that they are made by *you*, makes them more powerful.

A chant is halfway between a song and a poem. Nursery rhymes are like chants – they are half spoken and half sung, and you can make nursery rhymes into a chant quite easily. Fairy folk, elementals, and even angels enjoy chanting, and just singing a chant softly can bring these spiritual beings closer to you. Chants make good lullabies to send you to sleep, or you can use them simply because you feel especially happy that day.

Chant One

Sing a song of silver, a sixpence (ten cent) in my shoe.
If I sing it three times my wish will soon come true.

Chant Two

Sing a song on Monday, and a letter will come soon.
Sing again on Tuesday, a blessing to the moon.
Sing a song on Wednesday and you may lose a bet
Sing again on Thursday, if a present you would get.
Sing a song on Friday and go without a meal.
Sing again on Saturday, if a quarrel you would heal.
But if you sing on Sunday, you bless the rising sun.
Good luck will follow through the days until the week is done.

Chant Three

Hail moon, sail moon, across the silver sea,
Take from me a message to one who waits for me.
Tho' the sea divides us, to you I will be true,
When at last your ship comes in, life will begin anew.

Chant Four

Ten of heaven's angels standing in a line,
One of them did tell a lie and then there were nine.
Nine of heaven's angels passing through a gate,
One tripped and fell to earth and then there were eight.
Eight of heaven's angels came down to visit Devon,
One liked it so he stayed, and then there were seven.
Seven of heaven's angels were trimming all the wicks,
One burnt his fingers, ouch! Then there were six.
Six of heaven's angels, very much alive,
A comet carried one away and then there were five.
Five of heaven's angels sitting on the floor,
One of them he fell asleep and then there were four.
Four of heaven's angels standing 'neath a tree,
One of them began to climb and then there were three.
Three of heaven's angels wondering what to do,
One of them gave up his wings and then there were two.
Two of heaven's angels sitting in the sun,
One of them went off to swim and then there was one.
One of heaven's angels sitting all alone,
Decided he had had enough,
So then God called him home.

Dance

Dance is also part of magical training, mostly circle dancing. For this, everyone joins hands and circles round and round. Then one person moves inside the circle, taking those following with her or him. This leader circles inside the outer circle, and with each complete round they move further in, making a spiral. When the centre is reached, they turn and go the other way, unravelling the spiral until they are once more a circle.

In another type of circle dance, the dancers face alternately one into the circle and one facing out. Then each 'team' dances in opposite ways – clockwise or anti-clockwise. Or, again, the dancers can make two lines that move away from each other and then back again, making a wave-like motion.

Dancing in circles like this imitates the movement of the earth around the sun and, by echoing the solar movement, place the dancers 'in orbit' so that they join in the great dance of the planets around the primal life-giver. This is also why we circle round an altar in ceremonial magic, or around the fire in pagan worship.

Even in modern ballroom dancing, we still circle round the dance floor as dancers did in ancient times. Dancing round the Maypole, at Easter, Morris dancing and the Mummer's parade are memories of the past, when the old ways were still honoured. We still choose a May Queen to be crowned with flowers on village greens here in England, as we have done for hundreds of years. And a few churches still hold the custom for the vicar to lead his parishioners from the church and round the churchyard in a solemn dance to welcome the Spring.

All pagans love to dance at their meetings, usually in a circle and holding hands to symbolise our togetherness. At the changing of the seasons, we dance to express the meaning of the season through movement and sing as we dance. In olden times, each season had its own dance and a song to go with it. You will find examples of these further on in the book. These chants, dances, and songs are all that remain of the days when the earth was young.

It is up to people like you to carry them on and teach them to your children in turn.

Spring Chant (circa 1790)

Dance and leap in a circle, holding hands high to imitate the corn growing. First clockwise, then changing direction. At *down, down, down*, let your hands hang down.

Up, up, up comes the young Green Man,
From way down deep in the earth.
And up, up, up come the young green shoots,
As the corn seed comes to birth.
All winter long he has lain asleep,
But now he will come again.
The wheat will become our daily bread,
So we dance with might and main.
Up, up, up we will leap so high,
As high as the corn can grow.
And down, down, down will the reapers cut,
And we'll eat what we did sow.

Summer Chant (1750)

This is known as a processional dance. Boys and girls dance in pairs with joined hands, walking six steps, then dancing in a circle, another six steps and another circle and so on. Usually the whole village would join in and circle the boundaries.

The Summer Queen she walks the land
With flowers in Her hair.
She blesses all the growing things,
For they are in Her care.
The daisies follow in Her step
And bloom as She does go.
And we will follow in Her wake

And dance with heel and toe.
She brings us joy in summer's time
When days are warm and long.
And we do bless the Summer Queen
With laughter and with song.

Autumn Chant (1800)

A processional sung at harvest time, following the last wagon of corn to be gathered. Everyone gathered round a bonfire to toast the Harvest King.

Heigh Ho, the reapers go,
hear the scythe blades sigh,
up and down the fields they mow
with the gleaners moving nigh.

Heigh Ho, the stooks they grow,
and the wain is filling fast
The horses strain with might and main,
and noon comes by at last.

Heigh Ho, we bend down low,
to bind the stooks full tight
We lift and stack till bones do crack
from morn to the last daylight.

Heigh Ho, for those who sow,
when the planting time comes round.
When the corn grows high then the king must die
in the last stook he'll be bound.

Heigh Ho, when the king does go,
for he goes to feed us all,
When the corn is ground, he'll be nowhere found
but bread will be for all.
Heigh Ho, for the harvest home,
when all is gathered in,

when the cold wind moans
we will warm our bones
and give toast to the Lammas king.

Winter Chant

This is danced in a circle round a fire, starting slowly and getting quicker.

Hail the fire, the leaping flame,
see it dancing, ne'er the same.
Hand in hand we circle round,
what is lost can now be found.
The lady's grace doth fill the heart,
we merrie meet and merrie part.
Hand in hand we circle round,
marking out our dancing ground.
Quick and quicker dance the feet
fast and faster the heart doth beat.
Hand in hand we circle round
by the flame we all are bound.
Hail, hail, hail the sacred fire.

The tunes to these chants were never recorded. They differed from village to village and each had their own tune. People lived in close communities and gathered round a central fire. Everyone brought something to share. Here are three of the recipes from that time.

Harvest Nobbins (1870)

Crusty homemade bread rolls, with cheese and chive filling, or thin sliced beef. Some just plain with 'Noggin' Butter (butter mixed with rum). Each roll had a twist of straw around one end. Bowls of salted goose or pork dripping were provided to dip the Nobbins in. The straw prevented fingers from getting too greasy.

Dolores Ashcroft-Nowicki

Yimminy Tarts (1870)

Pastry cases baked blind with separate lids. After baking they were filled with stewed mixed fruit cooked with a little water. Before the lid was put on a spoonful of brandy mixed with honey was dribbled over the filling.

Honey Flaps

Squares of pastry spread first with honey, then with a mixture of nuts and dried fruit that had been well soaked in cider. Flaps were then closed, with all ends to the middle, and sealed with an apple ring. Then quickly baked in a very hot oven.

Chapter Seven

Angels, Elementals and Nature Spirits

As you get older, and if you are still interested in it, you will begin to learn more and more about the ancient art of magic. One of the things you will need to know about is the importance of direction. The quarters – East, West, North and South – are a living part of magic and cannot be ignored. Each one is linked to an angelic presence, as well as an elemental one, and both are linked to humankind by the fact that we all carry within us the four elements of earth, water, fire and air.

Angels and elementals don't need bodies like ours, as they exist in a different dimension, but they take the forms we give them in our imagination. This is why pictures of angels and elementals are shown in so many ways. They understand it is hard for us to think of them without a form. We don't know what they are really

Dolores Ashcroft-Nowicki

made of, but they will adapt to whatever form or shape we think up. Neither do angels come as girls or boys, though they can be thought of as either or both.

Let's go through the quarters and learn their names and powers. Almost all magical work begins with the east, though there are some ceremonies that use other quarters.

The East

Mostly we use east first as it is the place where the day begins, and the light returns to the world. The angel most connected to the east is Raphael who is a healing angel and is also linked to the element of air. Look at pictures of angels on the internet and see if one of them pleases you, then that can be the shape Raphael will take when you call the name. This angel is good to call on for help if you are ill.

Also in the east is the elemental king of air whose name is Paralda. He can be imagined as a tall man, wrapped in a cloak made of mist that moves all the time as if caught in a wind. His feet are winged and there are small wings each side of his head. He rules all the winds, from hurricanes to summer breezes. He likes to laugh and sing. But you can imagine him any way you like. He has many powers that you can learn about as you get older.

The power of the east is to bring in the new day, to open our eyes and minds to the world about us, and help us to start new things, have new ideas, and learn something new every day. When I am writing I like to imagine Paralda standing behind me helping me to find the right words. You might like to 'see' him as a bird – an eagle flying high and catching the wind in his wings. His children are called *sylphs*.

82

The South

The next direction is south and here the angel is called Michael. He is usually shown wearing armour and is often seen as heaven's General. His work is protective, and he leads an army of special angels. In fact, you might look on them as heaven's 'Special Forces Unit'.

Here the elemental king is called Djinn (say it like gin), and his power is that of fire in all its aspects, which can mean anger, fear and, like Michael, protection. In ancient times, when humanity first discovered how to make fire it was used as a protection at night to keep wild animals away from their sleeping place. Then they learned to cook food and, even later, used it to make clay pots stronger and to forge metal. But fire can be dangerous, and you must be careful with this element when working magic. Djinn rules the time of noon, or midday, when the sun is at its highest and hottest point. His children are called *salamanders*. Imagine Djinn rather like the genie in the story of Aladdin or Ali Baba and the forty thieves.

The West

Now we come to the west where we find the angel Gabriel. He is a messenger, like Hermes or Mercury in Greek legends, and was the angel who told Mary, the mother of Jesus, she would have a very special baby boy. Gabriel also guided the Three Wise Men to Bethlehem in the story of Jesus's birth. The west holds the power of water, so it controls things like creativity, dreams, and tides of both the sea and of life itself. The elemental king of water is called Nixsa and his children are called undines, but people also call them mermaids and mermen.

You will learn in school that life on earth began in the sea and without water nothing can live. We carry a lot of

Dolores Ashcroft-Nowicki

water in our bodies. In fact, everyone carries all four elements inside them, which is why they are honoured in magical work. We eat what grows in the earth, we drink the water, we breathe the air and our bodies regulate our temperature, so we can feel both heat and cold.

The North

The final direction is north and belongs to earth. The angel here is called Uriel and often carries a basket of fruit and flowers. The elemental king of earth is called Ghob (say it as Gobe.) You can imagine him as a much taller gnome. He is round and jolly and wears leather britches and sleeveless vest over a woollen shirt, strong sturdy boots and carries a shovel. He wears a beard and jokes and laughs a lot. He rules the kingdom of the gnomes and keeps them busy. Gnomes are also very inquisitive and like to borrow things. When you lose something that you had a moment ago, it is nearly always a gnome that has picked it up. When I lose something, I always ask Ghob if the gnomes have it and, if so, will they please give it back. (They especially like small coins like pennies.)

I find that if you fill a small box with bits and pieces, such as empty cotton reels, an old comb, a broken piece of jewellery, small things you no longer need, and leave it in a corner of the room or inside a wardrobe, and tell Ghob it is for the gnomes, you will not lose things so often. They love to mend things and use them for themselves.

The power of the north is the power of growing things and plants and trees grow tall and strong if they have enough to drink. They push their roots deep into the earth where the water is clean and pure.

Always remember to offer a blessing to all the elementals when you work with them. It means a great deal to them and they will work hard for you if they know you will bless them. Personally, I always offer a blessing to both angels and elementals before going to sleep.

Spirits of Nature

Besides elementals, there are many other beings who share the world with us. We may not always see them, but they are there, and they have their own kind of work. Every tree has a spirit called a dryad – they are very shy and seldom seen, but they follow the same cycle as their trees. They wake up in spring and begin to call up the sap in the tree's veins, where it has been sleeping. They make sure the leaf buds are in place to unfurl when the days get warmer. They love to dance with the wind and the air spirits (sylphs) and enjoy being touched gently.

Banks of wild flowers often have a being that shares energy with them and acts as a guardian. Gardens are full of these kinds of beings whose work is to make sure the flowers reach their full time of blooming. When you pick flowers to take into the house, it is much appreciated by these beings if you let them know what you want to pick, and you leave a blessing afterwards. That may sound silly, but everything around you is part of a living community. Their consciousness may not be as deep or as complex as yours, but they can feel joy and sorrow as we do.

The biggest and most aware of these beings are called devas and they look after whole stretches of the landscape that are especially beautiful and much admired. When standing in a place like this, you can feel their presence, and even join with them in their joy at simply *being* there. Witches and people like them are very aware that everything around us is alive in some way. Some are very slow in their 'thinking' – stones, cliffs, sacred circles, standing stones and such things – but they hold power within themselves. Mountains are full of power and are more acquainted with human beings who love to climb them. But some of the really big mountains do not like being climbed, they prefer to be alone and only talk to the great wind beings that live on and around them. As you learn to understand that everything around you is alive in some way, you will grow into a person the Earth Mother will know and love.

Let's talk about Fairies. There are as many different kinds as there are kinds of people. Most people think they don't exist except in fairy tales. But that is because they think 'existing' means being like them. But fairies are not like us, they 'exist' in a different way. The little particles that make up their 'bodies' are much finer than ours, so they are difficult to see. They are a very different kind of life form. But, if you forget all the scientific words explaining that, and accept that there are life forms that are not like yours and mine, you can begin to 'sense' their presence. You don't have to *see* things to know or feel that they are there. If you talk to them as if they *were* there, they will respond with thoughts, ideas, and pictures in your head, and if you are really lucky, you might get a sight of them now and then. But as always, you need to keep things like this to yourself. A witch must know how to keep secrets.

Fairies, like people, come in different forms. There are the very small ones, who are winged and look after the flowers, bushes and small wild creatures. There are bigger ones that can be mischievous and are not always friendly (sometimes they are even known to attack humans.) They tend to live inside the hills and smaller mountains where they feel safe from the outside world. Then there are the elves, almost as tall as us and very wise. They are the *old ones*, many of whom were here before we were. They seldom communicate with us and live in a world that seems to be a shadow one to ours. This book is not the place to explain further but understand that there are beings who occupy the same space as our world but in what we call another dimension.

Then there are beings who have been left over from another time, one when the earth was very new, and Mother Nature was trying out different forms to see which were the best. We hear about them in old stories of that time. They often wore forms that were half animal and half human. There are the centaurs, with the body of a horse and the top half of a human being. Fauns are quite small, almost childlike, and they have the legs and feet of a goat with little horns peeping through their hair.

The greatest of all these beings was the Great God Pan. In far off times, he lived in a part of Greece called Arcadia and he was the guardian of the wild creatures. He was always ready to help and protect them. But, because new ideas came into the world, he began to be seen as something that was not good, and people were taught to forget him. But he still exists in our hearts and minds, and although he is very seldom seen, he continues to look after the wild creatures. If you have read a book called *The Wind in the Willows* by Kenneth Grahame you will remember him as the one who found the baby otter when he was lost and kept him safe until his parents found him again.

The world you and I live in holds many secrets and many other forms of life. Most people have forgotten them and will tell you that they don't really exist, but this world is not the only one; there are many worlds to learn about, and these other beings have mostly gone to live there rather than here, where they are no longer believed in.

Most children are taught to think of them as just being characters in stories. If you are reading this book, you are one of the lucky ones, whose parents want you to know and remember the old ways and the old times when these beings shared the world with us.

When adults talk of the imagination, they usually mean day-dreams, but all witches know that the imagination is really a door into other worlds and other times. You can learn to explore them, *but* you must always understand that you have to come back into this world where you belong. You cannot stay in that other world for too long or you will become dissatisfied with this one and unable to be happy here. Visit the other worlds, by all means, but remember that this world is where you need to be.

Chapter Eight
What is a Ritual and What Does it Do?

A ritual, which some people call a ceremony, is a sort of *party* where you make a special place clean, tidy and pretty and then invite *beings* from the other world to come and be with you for a while. That sounds very strange, doesn't it? But as you have learned, there are other worlds and other kinds of beings, and a ritual or ceremony allows you to be together for a while. Rituals done by adults often have a more serious purpose, but the ones you will learn are just about being with family.

You can ask your parents and/or other family members to help you until you feel able to do it all by yourself. It's important to remember that some adults, especially teachers, don't always understand our kind of ritual, so don't talk about rituals to everyone.

A ritual can be done anywhere, no matter how small, as long as the circle has been cast and made clean, and the quarters have been opened. All ritual must have a purpose. The ones done by adults are often long and elaborate, but yours will be shorter and simpler.

A ritual is a special time and place where the two worlds can meet for a while, and where you can send blessings and good thoughts as gifts to those *other beings*. One of the nicest things about ritual is that you can send angels, or elementals, or fairies *thought presents* that become real presents as they cross over into the other world. This kind of 'get together' brings both worlds closer during that time. I have written two rituals for you to do: One is to contact angels and the other is for elementals, and includes the nature spirits, fairies, and *other* folk.

Contacting does not mean that they actually arrive and stand in front of you. It means the *essence* or the *feeling* of them being close to you, can be very real and might make you feel a little light headed. Angels have a special form in their own world, but in our world, they accept the form we have come to know from pictures. But when they are close, their presence can be felt. It will take a while, but you will soon be able to feel when they are around.

Grown-ups often have a special room or sacred place where they work ritual. But you are a beginner, so you do not have such a place yet. But, if you have a room of your own, or a place in the open where you can be quiet and not interrupted, then you can at least learn the basics and begin to understand the why, the where and the how of ritual and magical ceremony.

First, you must clear a space in which to work. This may mean tidying your room! You need a space big enough for you to lie down with your arms and legs spread out like a star. Mark the centre with a small table or a box tall enough to reach your waist. This will be your altar, so move it until the flat sides point to the Four Quarters. Over this place a white cloth.

In the centre there should be a candle, but fire is always a risk, especially if your robe has wide sleeves. There is a saying in magic that helps when you don't have what you need: *When in doubt, make do, because Intent is everything in magic.* So instead of a candle, use a torch. The candle symbolises light but so does the torch when it is lit. So, stand it upright in the centre, or balance it in a glass so that the light shines upward. On the altar, place your magical tools; the wand in the east, the sword in the south, the cup filled with water in the west and the pentacle in the north. You can also put a plate with some seeds on it in the north, or even a saucer with some earth, or a flower. Take a small handful of salt and carefully sprinkle it around the circle you have marked out but make sure you have everything you need with you before you do this.

You must understand that some people will say magic is wrong, or evil. Remember what I said about magic in the first chapter? All new things start out being magical. A seed becoming a flower is magical, a doctor removing an appendix is magical, reaching out to beings of another nature, angelic or elemental, is magical. These beings do not come to you of their own accord; you must invite them. 'Ask and you will receive' is quoted in the Bible, but people get upset when they ask and don't receive, then claim that magic does not work. But there is always the chance that if you get what you asked for, it may arrive with a lot of trouble. You might ask for money and the next day find a bag filled with money on a bus seat.

But it's not *your* money; someone may need it to pay an important bill. If you keep it, you are in deep trouble. But you got what you asked for. You will get better results if you ask for what you *need*, rather than what you *want*.

Ritual gathers power together in a specially prepared place, and then you must make absolutely certain what you want. Remember the shoes? Again, you might ask for money, and someone gives you a present of a Monopoly game, which comes with toy money. You did not specify *real* money. You must also make sure that you want that money to be yours to keep. It is no good finding a wallet and having to give it back to its owner.

You see, magic does not have a brain of its own – it is just power. It finds exactly what you ask for, but it doesn't bother about details.

In the next chapter you will find two rituals written specially for you. They are not very long, or complicated, but contain all you need to know at this point. The first deals with opening the quarters and calling the archangels and elemental kings. It is a sort of introduction ritual, so you can get to know these beings and make them aware of you as someone beginning to work magic. The second ritual is different and deals with you and the world around you. As you get older, you will take part in many different kinds of ritual. Eventually, you will reach a point where, believe it or not, you will find you do not need a ritual to contact the beings of other worlds and dimensions. You will become so used to their presence that just a thought, or a greeting, is enough. Our world is full of unseen presences all going about their own business, but you will be aware of them.

Chapter Nine
Casting a Circle and Greeting the Quarters

All magical work, with a few exceptions, is done within a circle of protection. This is to contain or hold any power from leaking out into unprepared space. Magical power is tricky and slippery stuff. Unless it is held securely it can cause trouble; accidents are more likely, it can cause things to go wrong and generally be a nuisance to everyone around. *Magical power has no consciousness of its own. It just does what it is told to do and keeps on doing it until told to stop.* This is why spells should end with: 'three times three' or 'so mote it be'. This gives the spell instructions to stop after a set time. The words 'so mote it Be' simply mean *'my will is done, finish...'*

Casting a circle is easy and should be done before you begin a ritual, spell, or any magical work. Exceptions can be when a spell is directed towards a chosen point, place or person, or if it is a healing spell. Then, an imaginary line of light is visualised leading from you to that person, usually by means of a photograph or something they have worn.

A circle of salt will provide protection for anything simple. For stronger work, you need to cast a circle and then do your work within it, leaving the circle only when all power has been dismissed. Usually you would wait to do this until you are older and more experienced, but it is something you need to know and practice. In the preceding chapter, you learned a circle casting spell, which is another way of making things safe. You speak the casting spell and, as you do, you turn clockwise, holding out your wand and drawing an invisible circle around you.

Always cast a circle bigger than you think you will need, if this is possible. For instance, while standing still and holding out your wand at arm's length, you need to imagine the circle at double the distance from where you are standing to the end of the wand. Measure it out before you begin and put something to act as a marker at the furthest point.

Work by the four directions, dedicating and opening each one, in order, as you circle round. At each point build an imaginary door or gate and call in a particular power or angel to guard it. Greet the guardian by name and give it directions. Always work clockwise when you are making your circle, beginning in the east with the powers of air. When you have completed your ritual work then, and only then, go around anti-clock wise and close each gate, thanking its guardian and offering a blessing. Again, I warn you that this is not something you can show to school friends or do where everyone can see you. Though it is no longer against the law to be a witch, or practice it as a religion, there will always be someone who thinks it is wicked and complains about it. Always keep in mind that as a witch you owe it to all witches to keep your magical work secret from those who don't understand it.

Why do we cast a circle? To make it a place special and holy. Christians have churches, Jews have synagogues, Muslims have mosques, Hindus have temples. All of these sacred places deserve your respect at all times. But, because of the history of bad feeling between witches and people who can't accept *differences*, we still have to be careful and keep our ways secret.

Spells and chants do not need to be done in a circle. Dances are done in a circle anyway. But serious work like rituals and ceremonies need to be done inside a protective place. Gather all the things you may need and check your list carefully. If you cross the line once the circle is drawn, it destroys it, and any work already done is of no use.

You need a small folding table covered with a white cloth, a candle in a holder, your magical tools, an incense stick, bread on the pentacle, and a bowl of salt. As you are not old enough to have wine, something like cranberry or grape juice will do for the chalice. You will also need a small silver coin.

Please note all rituals *must* have a candle or light on the altar. This makes certain you are working with good intent.

All ceremonies and rituals must have a reason for doing them. You can't raise power and not give it somewhere to go or something to do. So a ritual must be *for* something. It can be an event like a festival or a special day. It can be for someone else, to heal, help, or pass strength of purpose to them. It can be to say thank you for something received, or because you want to say thank you to a being of power, like an angelic guardian, your familiar, or the dream troll. You might have a special friend, teacher or a relative who needs help in some way, and a ritual of blessing will give them strength and hope.

You don't have to do a ritual every day. In fact, they should be kept for special times in your life. When something is used too often, what makes it special can be drained away and then it won't work as well, or even at all. As you grow up, you will go through many occasions, both happy and sad. Think of them as markers; times when you learn something new and how to deal with that *something*. Growing up is one of the hardest things you can do, but it can also be the most wonderful time.

The Witch's Broom

So, back to the circle. I expect you have seen pictures of witches with a broomstick. In ancient times, it was said they used them to fly, like Harry Potter in the Quidditch games. I'm afraid that is not going to happen for you! But the broom is still a magical tool. A circle can be used inside or outside. Witches and pagan people often have a room set aside for their magical work, but this is not always possible. So, a broom is used to 'sweep away' the effects of what happens in the room during the day.

Old-fashioned brooms can still be bought in craft shops and sometimes in garden centres, but they are easy to make yourself. You need a bundle of twigs and grass all the same length, quite a big bundle. Some strong twine, a stick for the handle about the thickness of your thumb and some strong glue. You will need a grown-up to help you, as the broom handle must be cut from a tree or bush, and then cut again to a suitable length. Once you have the handle, shave off all the knobbly bits and the bark so that it is smooth. Lay out the twigs and grasses in a row. I like to make small bundles of them and tie them tightly with string. Then pack them around the handle in layers of three or four, according to how thick you want it to be. Make sure the handle is deep inside the twigs, about five or six inches. When you think it is thick enough, bind a piece of strong cotton several times around it and ask an adult to nail it to the handle with half inch nails. Then paste some glue over it. This will make it hold together. Let the whole thing dry overnight, then trim the twigs and grasses to the length you want. Paint over the glued part to make it neat, and then you can cover the handle with varnish. Make sure it is the right height for you to use. (You can see all this being done step by step if you search for how to make a witch's broom on You Tube.)

You need space to cast a circle, so clear as much as you can. If outside, find a piece of level ground. All you need should be made ready, check to make sure, and keep clear in your head what you are going to do. When you are ready to begin, face east and begin to sweep from the middle to beyond where the circle will be, using a steady rhythm. Below is the chant to go with the cleansing of the circle.

First Ritual – Greeting the Four Quarters

The intent here is to make the Powers of the Four Quarters (Angelic and Elemental) aware of you.

Equipment Needed:

Small Table
White Cloth
Centre candle in holder (or torch, if you're using one instead)

Dolores Ashcroft-Nowicki

Your magical tools: wand, sword, cup with water or juice. Pentacle or bowl with wild flower seeds in it. If seeds aren't available then use bread crumbs, which can be scattered for birds afterwards.

Say, while beginning to sweep, facing east:

Out from the centre, one two three,
Thus, I sweep with leaf and tree,
Nothing dark may linger here,
Only light both full and clear.
Out from the centre and into the wood,
Making space for all that is good.
Clearing the way for spirits of light
That we may see them clear and bright.

Out from the centre go shadows all,
This space be safe till the cocks do call.
Out from the centre goes all fear,
Naught can harm those light holds dear.
Blessed be the circle,
Blessed be we,
Blessed be this place now paid with a fee.

(Now throw a small silver coin far beyond the circle.)

The first three verses can be repeated, while you sweep outwards from each direction, until the circle is complete, using the last verse as a finale.

Place the broom at the starting point and take up the bowl of salt. Sprinkle salt around the edge of the circle you made with the broom as a second barrier of safety. As you go around, repeat this prayer:

Creature of Salt, by the Earth that rules thee,
Bless the barrier between the worlds,

That we may work in peace and love
With all beings of light.

Within this circle, you can do small ceremonies suitable for your age. Use it for special days, perhaps your birthday, New Year's Day, the first day of each month or season. The only requirement is permission from your parents. They are your guardians until you are grown and deserve your respect and love. Begin your ceremony with a greeting to the angels of each quarter and its elemental king.

To do this face the east, and with your wand trace the outline of a door in the air before pointing the wand into it. Say:

With love and goodwill,
I call upon the archangel Raphael
And invite that presence of light to be with me in this place.

Pause now and imagine a pillar of rose-coloured light appearing inside the eastern doorway.

Raphael, angel of the eastern gate, be welcome.

Bow to the angel.

With love and goodwill,
I call upon Paralda,
The elemental king of air to be with me in this place.

Imagine the tall windswept figure of Paralda, wearing a crown of stars, stepping through the door and standing by Raphael.

Paralda, Elemental King of Air, be welcome.

Bow to Paralda.

Put the wand back on the altar.

Now, pick up the sword and go to the south. Here, draw the image of a door in the air with the sword. Say:

With love and goodwill,
I call upon the archangel Michael
And invite that presence of light to be with me in this place.

Pause and imagine a pillar of flame red light appearing inside the southern doorway.

Michael, angel of the southern gate be welcome.

Bow to Michael.

With love and good will,
I call on Djinn,
The elemental king of fire to be with me in this place.

Imagine the figure of Djinn, dressed in his genie-like clothes and wearing a crown of fire, stepping through the door and standing by Michael.

Djinn, Elemental King of Fire be welcome.

Bow to Djinn.

Now, put the sword back on the altar.

Take up the cup, face the west and draw the image of a door with the cup. Say:

With love and goodwill,
I call upon the Archangel Gabriel
And invite that presence of light to be with me in this place.

Pause and imagine a pillar of deep blue light standing inside the western doorway.

Gabriel, angel of the western gate be welcome.

Bow to Gabriel.

With love and goodwill,
I call on Nixsa,
The elemental king of water to be with me in this place.

Imagine the figure of Nixsa, dressed in robes of blue and green and wearing a crown of oyster shells, stepping through the door and standing by Gabriel.

Nixsa Elemental King of Water be welcome.

Bow to Nixsa.

Replace the cup upon the altar.

Now take up the pentacle and go to the north. Draw the image of a door with the pentacle. Say:

With love and goodwill,
I call upon the Archangel Uriel
And invite that presence of light to be with me in this place.

Pause and imagine a pillar of grass-green light standing inside the northern doorway.

Uriel, angel of the northern gate be welcome.

Bow to Uriel.

With love and goodwill,
I call on Ghob,
The elemental king of earth to be with me in this place.

Imagine the figure of Ghob, dressed in a robe of russet brown and wearing a crown of autumn leaves, stepping through the door and standing by Uriel.

Ghob, Elemental King of Earth be welcome.

Bow to Ghob.

Replace the pentacle and stand by the altar, facing east.

This is now a sacred place, and you have invited eight powerful beings to be with you, so it is important you really understand what you are saying. This is your first time doing a real ritual, and though it will be very simple, make it as good and as meaningful as you can.

With the forefinger of your right hand, touch your forehead between the eyes and say:

Dolores Ashcroft-Nowicki

I am a being of Air
Touch the earth and say:
I am being of Earth.
Touch your right shoulder and say:
I am a being of Fire
Touch your left shoulder and say:
I am a being of Water
Bring your hands together and say:
I am filled and blessed by these elements and do bless them in return.

Face the east with your hands together and say:

Raphael of the Healing Hands, I ask for health of body and strength of will that I may make the most of my school work and my family life. If troubles should come, help me to overcome them and learn from them.

Paralda, King of the Element of Air, help me in my school work that I may understand the lessons. Help me to guard my tongue that I may not offend by word or deed, to learn from mistakes and make allowances for those who would speak against me. Stand before me that I may see you both as examples to follow.

Go to the south with your hands together and say:

Michael, Angelic Warrior, teach me to accept what trials may come and to ride out the storms of life with courage. Stand beside me when I need strength. Help me to stand up for others when there is need. Show me that to attack is not always the right thing, but to seek the ways of peace.

Djinn, King of the Element of Fire, teach me that angry words are as deadly as arrows, and to hold my anger in check. Show me that emotions can be both a sword and a shield, and how to be a friend to those in need. I ask you to be a pattern in my life.

Go to the west with your hands together and say:

Gabriel, Messenger and Bearer of Glad Tidings, help me to understand that troubles can often be lessons in disguise and to accept them with good grace. Teach me that a hand outstretched in friendship may be refused, but not to take offence, and keep trying. Teach me that laughter can heal, and that joy is doubled when shared.

Nixsa, King of the Element of Water, wash me clean of envy and lies. Bathe me in your element and let me not thirst for what is not mine.

Go to the north with your hands together and say:

Uriel, Seed-Bearer and Guardian of Mother Earth. Make me aware of what I can do to help the Earth Mother. Let me feel Her under my feet as I walk, let me hear Her voice in bird song and know Her tears when it rains. Let me feel the joy of a simple flower as it unfolds to the sun.

Ghob, King of the Element of Earth, help me to understand the value of growing things, that they are the younger life of earth and therefore my brothers and sisters. This ritual is now completed.

While still facing the north, say:

I ask a blessing upon Uriel, Archangel of the North, peace be between us, return to your own level.

Ghob, Elemental King of Earth, be blessed for this meeting, return to your own level.

Bow and make a gesture of closing the northern door.

Go to the west and say:

I ask a blessing upon Gabriel, Archangel of the West, peace be between us, return to your own level.

Nixsa, Elemental King of Water, be blessed for this meeting, return to your own level.

Bow and make a gesture of closing the western door.

Go to the south and say:

I ask a blessing upon Michael, Archangel of the South, peace be between us, return to your own level.

Djinn, Elemental King of Fire, be blessed for this meeting, return to your own level.

Bow and make a gesture of closing the southern door.

Go to the east and say:

I ask a blessing upon Raphael, Archangel of the East, peace be between us, return to your own level.

Paralda, Elemental King of Air, be blessed for this meeting, return to your own level.

Bow and make gesture of closing the eastern door.

Take up the candle (or torch) and say:

May the light shine on all levels, that all may be blessed.

Blow out the candle (or turn off the torch) and say:

The ritual is completed.

Knock on the altar three times and leave your sacred space.

Second Ritual – Offering to Mother Earth

You will need on the altar: a white cloth, the usual central light (a candle in a holder or a torch), a bowl filled with wild flower seeds mixed with some earth (preferably from the area where the seeds will be scattered.) You will also need an incense stick already smoking, a cup of water, and also a clean tissue.

You won't need your magical tools for this ritual. When you set up your altar, the light goes in the centre with the other things around it. The opening of the quarters is shorter. This ritual should ideally be done in early spring, in the place where the seeds will be sown, but if that is not possible, then it can be done indoors.

Stand facing the east. With your right forefinger draw the five-pointed star, that witches call the pentagram, in the air before you. Point into the centre and say:

By the power of the Pentagram,
I open the eastern gate,
And request the presence of Paralda,
The Elemental King of Air,
To help me in this ritual.

Move to the South. Repeat the Pentagram and say:

By the power of the Pentagram,
I open the southern gate,
And request the presence of Djinn,
The Elemental King of Fire,
To help me in this ritual.

Move to the West. Repeat the Pentagram and say:

By the power of the Pentagram,
I open the western gate,
And request the presence of Nixsa,
The Elemental King of Water,
To help me in this ritual.

Move to the North. Repeat the Pentagram and say:

By the power of the Pentagram,
I open the northern gate
And request the presence of Ghob,
The Elemental King of Earth,
To help me in this ritual.

Return to east, place your hands together and say:

Hail Paralda, King of the Element of Air. Fill me with the power of your breath that I may breathe life into the earth and the seeds.

Take a deep breath, draw it down into your lungs and hold it for a few seconds. Imagine it filling your whole body with its energy.

Go to altar, take up the incense stick, present it to the south, and say:

Hail Djinn, King of the Element of Fire. Fill me with the power of your internal fire that I may enliven the earth and the seeds.

Imagine a flame coming from the south and entering your heart, filling it with the heat of love. Bow. Replace the incense stick on the altar.

Take the cup and go to west. Hold out the cup and say:

Hail Nixsa, King of the Element of Water. Fill this cup with the creative power of water that I may feed Mother Earth and give life to the seeds.

Imagine a single drop of water emerging from the west and joining with the water already there, empowering it even more. Replace the cup on the altar.

Pick up the bowl of earth and seeds. Go to north, hold out the bowl and say:

Ghob, King of the Element of Earth, I bring an offering to Mother Earth, seeds to enrich Her, and make Her even more beautiful. Bless the seeds that I offer and let the earth that holds them be blessed.

Take the bowl to the altar and breathe over them, releasing Paralda's energy into the seeds. Wave incense over the seeds to release the warmth of Djinn. Pour some water into the bowl to begin the process of growth passed to you by Nixsa. Lastly, mix the earth and seeds together so that the blessing of Ghob fills them with strength to grow and cover them with a clean tissue.

Standing at the altar, face east and hold out your right hand. Say:
I offer a blessing to Paralda and give Air leave to depart.

Face south and hold out your right hand. Say:
I offer a blessing to Djinn and give Fire leave to depart.

Face west and hold out your right hand. Say:
I offer a blessing to Nixsa and give Water leave to depart.

Face north and hold out your right hand. Say:
I offer a blessing to Ghob and give Earth leave to depart. This sacred place is now closed.

Clear everything away and leave the place neat and tidy. As soon as possible, take the bowl of earth and seeds to your chosen place, dig down about two or three inches and scatter the seeds gently, then cover them up with earth again. If any water is left, pour it over the place.

A gift to Mother Earth like this, even if only given once a year, will increase the bond between you. This works especially well if the place chosen has been neglected and

Dolores Ashcroft-Nowicki

left to go wild. Instead of seeds, you can plant small bulbs, daffodils, bluebells, pansies or anything that will give colour and a sense of beauty to a place that needs it. This ritual can also be used in a garden when you are replanting in the spring, or planting things like bushes, roses, lupins or foxgloves.

Chapter Ten
The Four Seasons
Part One: Spring and Summer

Everything responds to the four seasons, whether animals, plants, weather, or humans, and each season has its own kind of power. In spring, the power is creative and full of promise. Seeds have been sown with the intent to grow and provide food, healing, colour, pleasure and beauty. Animals give birth to their young and there is feeling of *newness* in the world.

Traditionally, 21st March is said to be the official beginning of spring. But I like to keep it simple, so I personally take the first day of March to be the opening of springtime. There is no hard and fast rule, and it makes things easy to arrange.

Spring is the time when cattle are let out into the fields

after being in the barn during the cold winter months. Clocks are altered; the days lengthen, and the evenings begin to grow lighter. The weather patterns change, and people begin to respond to the warmer days. Winter clothes are put away, blankets and duvets are washed and hung out to dry in the spring winds. We feel lighter and more energetic. We want to be up and active outside rather than sitting by the fire. In fact, we are responding, like the plant and animal life, to the call of the earth to be up and doing, growing, changing, and creating.

Because witches are close to the heart of Mother Nature, we feel this call more than ordinary folk. It is a good time to start new things, make plans on how to use the long warm days that lie ahead. In wintertime, we like to be indoors by the fire and not using as much energy, but now there is a feeling of wanting to be out and about.

Magic is not just about spells, rituals, and magical tools, it is also about responding to the rhythms of the earth and using them to help you grow stronger and wiser. In winter, we sleep longer and heavier. In the spring, we begin to sleep less and wake up earlier, wanting to be up and doing things. By flowing with the earth tides, we work with the laws of the universe and not against them.

There are rituals and ceremonies especially for the spring tides, and they are mostly concerned with the growth of plants, animals and *you*. You grow physically bigger and stronger in the spring and summer. Your brain is more alert and able to understand and absorb knowledge quicker in the autumn and winter. That doesn't mean you can't learn in the spring, just that your mind and body is concentrating on growing bigger at that time. Exercise and fresh food help your body to prepare for the next winter when it comes.

Spring is a good time to learn the art of observing, because so much is happening around you, but few people, with the exception of those who work the land, notice this. Witches, however, look at the world as if it is a book to be read, and spring is the first page. To *observe* doesn't mean just looking around, it means looking, learning, understanding and being a part of what is happening day by day.

Magic is about being one with the world around you, and witches are in many ways guardians of the earth. Everything has a sense of being, and because witches understand that, they help to keep the world in balance. Learn to notice the small things that mark each season. Have you ever noticed the small grasses and flowers that grow where the side of a building meets the pavement? Basically, they are weeds, but they are alive and doing what they were meant to do, which is to grow and put out tiny flowers that no one really notices. But, though small, these plants are alive and doing their work. Just by stopping and noticing, you give them energy and when you give, you always get something in return. It may not be right away, but the energy you gave those tiny flowers will come back to you in a good way.

This is a part of magic that many people do not understand. Life and energy move in a circle. You give out and it is returned to you in different ways. Spring is the time when life energy wakes up from its winter sleep and begins to fill the world with its power. As you go to school, or shopping, or just playing with your friends, spare a moment to see if you can find something you have not noticed before. There are things to do, see and learn, and everything and everybody is a part of it. It is a magic that happens every year.

Dolores Ashcroft-Nowicki

Spring

Spring rituals are about preparing for summer. Summer prepares for autumn and autumn for winter. A circle of power, growth, renewal, learning and the exchange of energies. See how many things you can discover. Look at the tree branches and see the tight leaf buds getting ready to unfurl. Look for the first sign of green showing above ground in gardens and fields. Look in a mirror and see that *you* have changed; the shoes you bought are starting to pinch, your school skirt is too small, trousers need their hems letting down. Growing is magic that happens to us all, and spring is responsible.

Spring is celebrated with different traditions and symbols, but some symbols are worldwide. The main one is the Easter egg, followed by the Easter bunny (rabbit) and the hare. Real eggs are painted in bright colours and hidden around the house, and in the garden, for children to find. In Greece, they are carried around and people gently knock their eggs together while saying, 'Christ is Risen'.

Eggs are a symbol of birth and renewal. There is a Latin saying *'Omne vivum ex ovo'* which means *'all life comes from the egg'*. Some people keep a special candle called *the pascal,* which is kept burning all Easter day. Whatever tradition you follow, spring holds a belief in life awakening after its winter sleep. Noticing things will become a habit, and your awareness of the world will increase. You might like to use a ritual I do every year. The island where I live has many stone circles, standing stones and Neolithic remains. On 1st March, I fill a jug with milk and honey and go to one of the circles and sprinkle the stones with the mixture to bless them. While I do this, I say the following:

Blest be the hands that raised these stones.
And saw them as the Earth Mother's bones.
Blest be those who worshipped here,
And blest be the Goddess they held so dear.
I offer milk to their souls reborn,
To welcome the sun on spring's new dawn.
Honey from the hive is offered free,
To sweeten the link twixt thee and me.
Ancestors all, I hold you dear,
Accept the offering now made here.

May Day

In May we have the Maypole, which is still put up on many English fields and decked with ribbons for everyone to dance with. In Helston, a small town in Cornwall, they celebrate the *Furry Dance,* when ladies wear long dresses and the men wear top hats and tails and they dance through the streets to a special tune.

The Helston Furry Dance

www.abcnotation.com/tunes

Dancing around the Maypole is a very ancient ritual and has been celebrated in different countries for thousands of years and in different ways.

The selection and crowning of a *May Queen* is another ancient practice. Traditionally, the prettiest girl in the village is chosen and, crowned with flowers, is carried through the High Street by the young men, on a chair decked with flowers, ribbons and leafy branches. She is given gifts, and the young men sing songs and read poems to her. For a whole week, she is the most important person in the village.

Spring Protection

In spring, take a twig from an oak, an ash and a hawthorn. Ask for permission from the trees to do this and give them some water as a fee.

With the buds just showing green, bind them three times three with red thread. Hang this over the front door and chant:

Oak and thorn and bright ash tree
Bring through my door good luck for me.
Oak and ash and sharp old thorn,
Bring good health with each new dawn.
Thorn and ash and strong oak tree,
Guard house and home and the family.

Summer

Now we come to summertime. Spring was a busy time, planting, sowing, weeding, seeing to fields and gardens and planning ahead. It was all to do with preparation. Now comes summer, with its long hot days and now there is time to relax and enjoy the seasonal celebrations. There are many of these throughout the whole year, too many to go into here, but I will tell you about the most important ones. One of these is called Beltane. Sometimes this is spelt in the old Celtic way of Bealtaine. It begins on the last evening of April and lasts through the night into the 1st of May.

In one sense, this celebration is a wedding. May and June are considered to be wedding months, when days are long and warm, and everyone can wear their best clothes. Beltane, in the ancient days, was the time when the *Spring Maid*, the Goddess of Spring, was married to the *Horned Lord*, or *The Herne*, who ruled the forest and the wild creatures. His crown of stag horns proclaimed his right to make the goddess his wife. In many celebrations this was, and still is, a ritual enacted each year. It usually begins at sunset and goes on through the night. Songs, dances and feasting are all a part of the celebrations.

In England, there are wrestling matches and special songs and dances, and bonfires are lit on the hills. The spelling of bonfire in the old way is *bonefire*, because these special fires were always built on two animal thigh or leg bones crossed, rather like the bones on the pirate flag. In fact, that might have been the origin of the skull and cross-bones. The meaning of many of these ancient ways and symbols has been lost, but we still continue to honour them.

As you get older, and you read more about the old ways, you will find there was a darker side to them, for the world was a harsher place back then. Today we celebrate the same festivals but with a lighter heart and a different emphasis.

Midsummer

21st June is Midsummer's Day, the summer solstice. This is the longest day in the year and the turning point, when the celebrations have a touch of sadness, for the nights then begin to draw in. It is celebrated with bonfires and feasting. But soon the days will get shorter and the sun will seem cooler, so everyone makes as much of the remaining summer as they can. Each village had its way of marking the midsummer point in the year, but it was always a feast day when food and drink was shared by all.

Animals eat as much as they can during the summer months because food will be scarce when winter comes. We are animals as well, so in the past it was customary to eat well when food was plentiful and build up strength to last the winter. Nowadays, we can store food and have no need to stuff ourselves, but old habits die hard, and we still tend to feast during the summer

These celebrations are based on old English traditions. The craft – witchcraft – is the oldest of all traditions, since the day that the first person thought of thanking the earth for their food. It has many names in many countries and just as many ways of being practiced. The way it is worked in Africa is not as it is done in Romania, France, Spain or the USA. I was taught first by my grandmother, then years later I became *The Last Walker*. The very last purely craft village was dying and would soon be engulfed by a housing estate and enclosed in a fast-growing city. I was asked to spend that last year learning and recording their ancient ways. Therefore, my idea of the craft is perhaps one of the oldest, and I treasure it and teach it to others. When America opened its doors to the world, those who entered brought their own ways with them. And taught them. Those who came from Britain brought the one of the oldest traditions, and that is what I teach. It is not always the same as how others might teach it, but it is offered with love and with respect.

Pagans in America have developed their own festivals and celebrations, which are more numerous than the English. So look for, and read about, the pagan ways in your area. Traditions and beliefs grow and change but they always have a common link to bind them.

Ritual for Midsummer's Day

Gather sprigs of different flowers, especially roses and herbs. Lay them on a cloth on the grass and let the sun dry them. Then steep them in water overnight. Afterwards, put the water into a bowl. Sprinkle this water all around the garden on 21st June and invoke the angel of gardens to bless all the growing things. In the evening, take what's left into your bedroom and light a rose-coloured candle. Wash your hands and face in the water and say a prayer to the angel Uriel for good fortune. Then sleep. Next day, pour any water left over the garden.

Lammas

One of the most important days in summer is the festival of Lammas, which falls on 1st August. It was once a day of sacrifice, but now, although it is no longer what it once was, the idea behind it still needs to be understood. In a way, it shares a link with the Christian faith. The Corn King is an ancient symbol and has had many names down the years. As the corn is cut to make bread, the old belief was that a man was chosen to be the Corn King and, when the corn was harvested, he too would be 'harvested,' giving his life to the earth as the corn gave its life to be ground into flour.

The Lammas King, or Corn King, was 'cut down' on the first day of August. The word Lammas is thought to come from 'loaf mass,' for the first loaf of bread made from the harvest was shared by the whole village. They believed it was sacred because of the sacrifice it had taken. It follows the idea that when you *give* with no thought of self, you set in motion a response that means you get something in return. In our time, we think sacrifice is wrong, but Jesus was a sacrifice, as many of the great teachers and saviours have been. Centuries ago people did not hold life as dear as we do today.

Abbots Bromley Horn Dance [Em]

Morris dancing is very popular in England and there are many versions. Some are done with swords and others with wooden batons. One man is usually dressed as an old woman (supposedly a witch) and another is the *Dark Man*, the *Man in Black*, the leader or high priest of the witches. Some dances go back to the tenth century and use special costumes. Except for the Abbots Bromley Horn Dance, which is performed in September, Morris dancing can take place at any time during the summer, but nearly always during Lammas week.

Stone Circles and the Ancestors

Stone circles were raised for many different reasons. Usually they marked the burial place of someone important, to make it sacred so that it could be used for special rituals, or to honour the ancestors. They can be found all over the world, but there may not be anything like that near you. You can build your own stone circle, or just one standing stone. This is called a menhir.

If you have a garden or know of a place that is quiet and

not visited very often, you can make a circle of stones to mark something or someone special. Witches honour their ancestors and remember them in their prayers and invocations. The stones don't have to be large; they can be as small as pebbles. A few chapters back, I told you that *intent* is important when working magic. So, you can begin by looking for special stones (or just one stone). It might be one you see and like because of its shape or colour. You might find it on a beach or in a forest when you are on holiday. It is important that you *feel* it is the right kind of stone. If you want to make a circle, each stone should be chosen because it *feels* right. They don't have to be the same shape, but it is better if they are a similar size.

How many stones should you use for a circle? Seven is a good number; it has six to make a balance and one in the middle as the focal point. *Or* you can have eight around the edge and add one in the middle to make nine. Both seven and nine are magical numbers. Decide where you are going to put them. Choose somewhere as private as possible and not too visible to other eyes. Make sure each one is rooted firmly into the earth. The centre one is important and must be chosen carefully. The circle can be small and still be powerful.

Once the centre stone is in place you can consecrate the circle to *the ancestors*. Ancestors are very important. They are the foundation of the family; we exist because they lived. Therefore, we owe them respect. Talent, looks, health, names, property, all stem from our ancestors. By building a circle and dedicating it to them we honour them and thank them for our existence. Stones last... so do ancestors. One day *you* will be an ancestor.

If you decide to use a menhir, just one stone, it can be

larger, but again placed so that it does not stand out. If it is in your own garden that will not be a problem.

Now comes the most important thing: once your circle is up, it *must* be kept free from weeds and rubbish. It *must* be used at least twice a year, spring and autumn, summer and winter. It can be used more often, of course, but if left forgotten, its power will seek out someone else to renew it. That might mean, for some reason, you may move from that house or location. You are old enough to understand that magic is *not* a game. It is a serious type of energy that can cause things to happen.

Ancient circles are often very big and tall. Yours will be much smaller and stand no taller than six to ten inches, but size does not matter as your *intent* means that when empowered they will be just as magical. You will see from the pictures above that they are not an exact circle. It may take a time to build yours, as each stone must be found and put into place, but that is the way magic works; it builds up slowly. Like you, it grows slowly but surely each year, getting taller and learning more of the world about you.

A stone circle like this represents your ancestors – the family members that stretch back into the past. They are the foundation, the basis of your family. The circle is a symbol of the close family ties, the stones represent strength and support. So, when anything important happens, you can go to the circle and tell the stones all about it. Slowly they will begin to send you support, love, strength and the ability to deal with problems. Each spring, autumn, summer and winter, sprinkle the stones with a little milk and honey. Wish them well at Christmas and New Year, and on Midsummer's Day. Places become magical and sacred because we see them and treat them as such. As I told you, everything has a sense of being something, and when we recognise that and acknowledge it, we increase its ability to know itself and its power, and it shares all that with us.

Chapter Eleven
The Four Seasons
Part Two: Autumn/Fall and Winter

Spring holds the power of beginning, creation, planning, and looking forward. Summer's power is that of growth, increase and ease of labour. Autumn's power brings fruitfulness, harvest, reward of hard work, thankfulness and sharing. Winter's power brings rest, the slowing down of energy, withdrawal and recovery, community spirit and celebration.

Autumn

Harvest festivals, Thanksgiving, and the sharing of the results of the year's work, makes autumn one of the most joyous, and at the same time, most anxious seasons. So much depends on the success of the harvest. Even if one's work is not concerned with the growing of food, so much depends on its bounty. Once again, we find the age-old idea of giving to others and receiving in our turn. During autumn, churches, chapels and holy places of all faiths hold special prayers and offer thanks. They also collect gifts of food to share with those who have none. The whole idea of harvest and thanksgiving is based on sharing with others. It is a time for families to come together and celebrate their closeness.

In pre-Saxon England, when there were still whole villages living the pagan way, it was a time when the old and those in need were given food stores for the winter. This would have included wood for their fires, flour for bread and wool to spin and weave into clothing. Winter can come early and last longer than usual, so as soon as the harvest was gathered in, it was time to preserve fruits and vegetables and dry the herbs. Old candle ends were melted to make new ones, and animal fats were also used for this purpose. Cheese and butter had to be made and mattresses stuffed with fresh straw.

Animals were inspected to decide which would be saved and which would be killed and preserved in salt against the coming winter. September, October and November were months of intense work to make sure there was enough food stored to see communities through the winter. We live in a time in a time when, if we run out of bread, milk, meat, eggs, we can go to the nearest supermarket and buy more. In ancient times, if you ran out of such things, you went without.

Once the harvest had been gathered in (the last sheaf was always raised on a pole and offered to the birds, who were seen as the messengers of the Mother Goddess) then the celebration of Harvest Home could begin. In the village where I learned my craft, autumn was also a time when the High Lord made a list of the outlying farms, where the elderly might need extra stores. Then what had been gathered – flour, cheese, preserves, salt, vegetables and sacks of potatoes, anything that could be stored – was stored and covered with sacking and straw, ready to be handed out if supplies ran low. Nowadays, even small villages can be reached in deep winter. But twenty years ago, winter was a difficult time and the people living in smaller, isolated places came together to share and help.

Autumn was also a time when those who lived in remote villages went into the nearest town and bought what they needed. Often the women had made things to sell during the year: lace, and hand crocheted blankets, embroidered cloths, jams, and jars of honey. While the men would carve wooden toys, spoons and bowls, or make leather belts and slippers. These were offered on street markets and the money made was used to buy winter supplies. Of course, I am talking about a time when I was young, and supermarkets had not yet appeared.

We still celebrate Harvest Home and Thanksgiving, and it is right to do so, because the Earth Mother has given us so much. In the old days, the pagan way was to return in kind. At harvest time, the wild creatures, who are also Her children, need to fatten up for the winter. So keep bird feeders filled up, put out cat food for hedgehogs, (*not* bread and milk as it will harm them), or anything that can help to keep the wild ones fed until the spring.

Mabon – the Autumn Equinox

There is also a second kind of harvest festival – the autumn equinox or Feast of Mabon. (Mabon is a figure from Welsh mythology, who in modern paganism has become the special god of the autumn equinox. His name means 'Great Son'.) The equinox falls around the 21st of September and, like the spring equinox, this is a time when day and night times are equal. It reminds us that we need to re-balance ourselves. As we went through the year, we may have done things we know to be wrong. We may have forgotten to do certain things, or not done them as well as we should. Most of all, it is a time to think about how we see ourselves. In ancient times, it was the custom in this season to pay back anything that was owed: money or work promised, or whatever we said that we would do for someone earlier in the year and didn't. Now is the time to make amends.

Autumn is a time to patch up quarrels, to tell friends how much they mean to you, to thank those who have been kind to you. I like to buy small boxes of chocolates and give them with a thank you card to people in certain shops where they always smile as they serve me. Perhaps you could do this for such people as the 'lollipop person', who guides you across the traffic, or a teacher who helped you solve a problem. Your gift or card has value because they do not expect it, and it makes them feel appreciated. Here is a simple ritual you can do, but because it involves candles and flame, *always* have an adult with you *or* do it as a family.

Mabon Ritual of Thanks

You will need a small table with a white cloth and a bigger than usual central candle with a golden ribbon round it. A wooden bowl filled with apple slices, cut horizontally so the star-shaped core can be seen, and a saucer of honey. Stand the centre candle in a saucer of salted water and have smaller candles, one for each person, in different colours on the table.

Gather everyone around and hold hands, as one person carefully lights the centre candle.

Bless the Mabon candle with the following words:

We offer thanks to Mother Earth
And Mabon, the Child of Light.
We call the four elements to this altar.
Salt of the earth, water, fire,
And the air of our breath as we speak our prayer.
We ask a blessing on this gathering,
For those we love who cannot be present,
For the ancestors from whom we descend,
And all on our planet and its many life forms.
May this time of plenty continue through the year.
May there be food for all
And may love prevail upon the earth.
May the five-pointed star,
Hidden in the apple of knowledge,
Show us the power of the fifth element of spirit.
So mote it be.

All reply: *So mote it be.*

Call each person in turn to the altar, light one of the candles and give it to them with a kiss of love and peace. Offer each person an apple slice with the words:

May the Spirit of Mabon be a flame within you.

The apple should be dipped in the honey and eaten. The idea was to *sweeten* your words throughout the coming year. The old ritual continues with the candles being carried through the house to fill it with light as the Mabon song is sung.

'All Hail, All Hail, the Child of Light
Who comes to lighten winter's night.
All weary travellers welcome be,
Who welcomes them doth welcome thee.

Dolores Ashcroft-Nowicki

Come share with us sweet Mabon's light,
For all are precious in his sight.
All hail, all hail, now guard us well
For what will come we cannot tell.
In thee we trust the spring to see,
Let there be love twixt thee and me.

The ritual ends with a glass of hot cider shared by all.

An unexpected guest at this time is doubly welcome, for they are seen as representations of Mabon.

Samhain

The other ritual for this time of year is *Samhain*. Say it in the Celtic way: *sow-ain*. Some people see it as the Day of the Dead, but not in a frightening way, for the old ones saw death as a new beginning. Nowadays, we see it celebrated as Halloween or All Hallows Eve – the time when the spirit world comes very close to our own. Children dress up as ghosts, witches, devils, imps, and all sorts of fancy-dress costumes, and go trick or treating around the neighbourhood. In some countries, all fires are put out and re-lit from a central *bonefire* lit on the village green. Pumpkins are hollowed out and candles put inside them to add to the light and chase away the darkness. It has become a modern celebration, but its ancient meaning still shines through. Torchlight processions are popular at this time, and in some areas, barrels of flaming tar are carried through the street. Not something I would recommend.

Some communities pack a supper and visit the family graves and celebrate their lives and memories. This can be frightening if you are very young, but the thing is to remember that those no longer with you on earth, are still with you in other ways. They will always be a part of you because they were – and still are – family. Memories are a way in which we can still be with them. This is a time when, for a short while, they can be close. For instance, think of a grandmother or grandfather who loved you but who isn't wearing a body anymore. That doesn't mean they no longer love you, or that they want to frighten you, they just want to see you and let you know they are watching over you.

You can still enjoy Halloween, and go trick or treating, but later when you are tucked up in bed you can remember your ancestors and even talk out loud to them. Don't feel silly doing this. Remember that everything in the universe is made up of vibrations (moving sound) so they will hear you, but in a different way. Spend a few moments telling them what you are doing at school, or what you want to do when you grow up. Remember to tell them you love them, because love is an energy that never dies and never goes away. It is not a good idea to have a lighted candle in a bedroom, but a small torch switched on and put in the window is a nice way to let those no longer with you in the world know that you remember them on Halloween night.

Ritual for Halloween

Scatter some corn seeds before the kitchen door before you go to bed and put down a bowl of water and a piece of bread. Call on The Black Dog guardian:

Black Dog, come and guard my soul,
Drink the water from the bowl.
Black Dog, come and guard my bed,
Eat your fill of the offered bread.
Black Dog, come and scatter the seeds,
May they grow and fill my needs.
In the morning, bury the bread, scatter the water and sow the seeds.

Dolores Ashcroft-Nowicki

Samhain Chant

(Always wash hands before doing magic.)

Water pure and water clear,
Magical as a mermaid's tear,
Cleanse my hands that they may weave
A spell of love this Hallows eve.
Let those now passed but still held dear,
Come close and know that we are near.
We bless your name and grant you light,
With love upon All Hallows night.

Yule and New Year

Now we come to winter, the last season of the year, the time of the Yule Log, the Longest Night, the Return of the Sun and, of course, the Christian celebration of Christmas. Although it is a time when the birth of Jesus is celebrated, it is highly unlikely he was actually born at this time. In fact, many other great teachers of different faiths were supposed to be born on 25th December: the god Mithras was also said to have been born in a cave at this time, surrounded by animals. The births of Krishna, Buddha, Frey, Adonis and Dionysus were all celebrated on this date. It is the time when the sun begins its journey back, so it represents light returning to brighten the world and *warm it up* once more.

One of the many pagan rituals was, and still is, the lighting of the Yule Log. This time is the turning point of the year, and the word Yule comes from the ancient word *hoel* meaning a wheel. There are many places in England where the Yule Log is placed on top of what remains of the previous year's log, which again was part of the one before that. In this way, the ancients believed that they kept the Wheel of the Year turning. I know of several areas where this practice dates back literally hundreds of years – with each log being lit on the remains of the one before it.

The ancient goddess Bride was, and still is, a fire goddess. Christianity made her into St Bridget, but her pagan power is still kept alive today. In Kildare, in Ireland, there is a convent where the sisters keep a sacred fire burning continuously. It follows a custom from the 12th century. The current fire was lit in 1993 and has never gone out since then. It seems that the Old Gods are still with us. Fairy lights displayed in windows, to guide those in need to a place of warmth and light, and light displays in houses and gardens, are ways in which the old traditions still make their presence felt.

In the far north, the fire festival of '*Up Helly Aa*' consists of the image of Viking Galley being built then set on fire. All this is accompanied by processions, contests, marches etc.

The last festival of the year, of course, is New Year's Eve, which leads into New Year's Day. This is a time when everyone makes new year promises to themselves:

'I will get up early and do some exercise.'
'I will do my homework as soon as I get home.'
'I will give up sweets during the week.'
'I will remember to write thank you letters for my Christmas presents.'

The trouble is that such well-meaning promises are short-lived and soon forgotten. The best way is to choose just one and, if you have brothers and sisters, help by reminding each other as you wake up in the morning. Having just one resolution is easier than making a whole list of them.

Dolores Ashcroft-Nowicki

As an only child, my father asked me every evening if I had kept my promise. At that time, we still had the old coins, with half-pennies, pennies and three-penny bits, and my pocket money was three pennies a week. (You could buy a chocolate bar for a half-penny then.) If I had done my homework right away, or polished my shoes for school the next day, he would add a half-penny. But if I had not, he would take the same amount away. I never knew until Saturday morning how much – or how little – I would get. It certainly worked for me, though there were many times when I only got a halfpenny (and one really good week when I got *four* pennies.)

Don't get down-hearted if you keep forgetting; trying is a good way to keep your promise in mind. Very few people, especially grown-ups, manage to keep their New Year promises. It takes discipline.

The word discipline means doing the things you don't like doing because:

★   It is necessary (like washing your hands before meals and cleaning your teeth at night.)
★   Because it makes things easier (prepare your school things before you go to bed, and you have five minutes extra in bed!)
★   It's good for you (like eating your greens or making your bed in the morning and tidying your room once a week.)

Discipline means doing things that *have* to be done, even if you'd rather not do them, and would prefer to play on the computer, or stay in bed on a cold morning.

Keep the garden clean and tidy; don't expect the gnomes to do it all. Sow wild flower seeds in the wood in spring or plant bulbs round an oak tree. Remember to celebrate seasonal rituals, even if they are done earlier or later because you are going to a party. As time goes on, there will be many things to learn and practice. Magic means you have two schools; the day-to-day one and the secret one only you know about.

Chapter Twelve
The Magical Diary.

As you grow, your mind also grows and changes. You will learn about the *you* that lives inside your head. It's not always easy to grow up. But look at each day as a page in a diary ready for you to fill with thoughts and ideas. What you don't want is a book full of blank pages.

At the beginning of this book, you saw a drawing of a little witch carrying a *big* book. This is a special kind of book and every *real* witch has one. Some call it a *Book of Shadows*, some call it *A Magical Diary* or *My Book of Spells*. I called mine *the Book of Images*. In this book, you can write all your thoughts and ideas – what you saw or felt in a ritual or while making a spell. What you learned during the day. You should keep a record of all the magical work that you do.

In this chapter, I will show you how to prepare a magical diary and give you some things to write in it. Write it by hand because that makes it more special. Remember it has to be a real book, not typed onto a computer or an iPad. If you write all the things you learn, you will soon fill up your diary, then seal it, put it away and begin a new book.

When you grow up, you may one day become a writer and write books everyone will want to read. Writing a book is an act of magic. Less than a hundred years ago, very few children could read or write. You are very lucky. And as an author you will be a *Story-Teller*, one of the oldest professions in the world. Writing stories is a way to invite people into your own magical inner world and share it with them for a while. It is also a way to preserve your thoughts, ideas, hopes, and dreams and one day to pass them on to your own children. You see, every real witch is a guardian of ancient knowledge that has been passed down for thousands of years. That makes you a special person, and a responsible one. There will come a time when you are so busy growing up that you may put aside what you are learning and reading right now. But knowledge like this is very patient: it will wait until the time is right, then it will wake up inside you and start working again. When that happens, your magical diary will be there waiting to be opened again.

When I was young there were no computers or Kindles, just books. Now, having access to a whole world of books at the touch of a button is amazing. However, there is nothing quite like the feel of a real book in your hands and the action of turning pages seems to add to the excitement of wondering what the next page will show.

Books are precious, for they hold in them the thoughts, ideas, hopes and dreams of those who write them. They can also be passed on to others, so those dreams can be thought about, and new ones added to them. When you are older, you might decide to learn more about being a pagan, and this kind of learning can last all through your life. As the years pass, you will get to know and understand many things and, more importantly, you will add your own thoughts and ideas to them.

We can still read and learn about the pagan way of life in ancient times because the pagans of that time wrote down what they did, how they did it and why. Traditionally, every witch has a book in which she or he records what they have done week by week. What they have learned, what rituals, spells, songs or dances they may have done or read about. What they did in each season as it happened. Most importantly they write down their thoughts and their dreams.

Such books are valued and passed down in pagan families. Just think how old some of them must be. Visit a museum and look at really old books. Think how difficult it would have been then, because they were written using a quill pen made from a bird's feather, and ink made from water and coloured powders. It took a long time to write just one page, but the writers knew it was important to keep their ways and beliefs recorded so that their children would be able to keep their ideas, songs, dances, and celebrations alive. As a witch, you can also help to keep those ancient practices thriving. You can add to them as you get older, recording your own ideas, songs, spells and memories for those who will come after you in the future.

An ordinary notebook will do, but you can ask for a strongly-bound notebook for a birthday or Christmas present. Don't get the usual kind of diary – you need one with blank pages so that you can write as much or as little as you need. These days you can buy them with a lock already in place. However, they are usually just pocket size so, if you can, find one that is at least ten to twelve inches square. On the first page write *My Magical Diary*. Underneath, put your name, age, birthday, and the date you began the book, and use a pen, not a pencil.

My father made me my first magical diary from an ordinary letter-sized notebook. He made front and back covers from cardboard, then made loops from an old leather shoelace so the book could be closed with a small lock. It was not elegant, but I loved it and recorded all the things I had done or thought about during the week. Things my Nanna taught me about herbs, the meanings of flowers, how to make corn dollies and how to make a spell. I wrote my first spells in that book and marked all the days that were special.

I wish I still had it, but it was lost as we moved from place to place during the War, so I had to rely on my memory. I made a spell to get it back, but it didn't seem to work, so I gave up. But I didn't understand that spells don't give up. If it is important, they keep working. Many years later, when I had children of my own, I visited a friend who was leaving for America. Like me, he collected books and he told me to take whatever I wanted. But one book he gave me as a personal gift. It was a very big and very old leather-bound ledger that had never been used. Just the thing for a *book of magical images*. I still have it and use it today.

Once you have your magical diary, write your magical name on the first page. Remember we talked about the importance of names at the beginning of the book. You can also put a photo of yourself there as well. One day, your grandchildren may open the book and say to *their* children: 'This was your great grandmother's book of magic.'

Your book should have a lot of pages, so you can divide it into sections like: Herbs, Seasons, Rituals, Moon and Sun Magic, Festival Days, Chants and Songs, Spells, Elementals and so on. Most importantly, it will have your day to day entries. Try to keep the same subjects and information together, it saves time.

So, first things first. Begin with the day and the date. How did you feel when you got up today? Happy? Sad? Did you see anything funny, strange or interesting on the way to school? Often the way you feel attracts things to you. I sometimes find pennies, nails, rubber bands and safety pins on the pavement. I think of them as gifts from the universe that might come in useful and always pick them up. Once I found a sea shell, which doesn't sound exciting, but it was in the middle of London and miles away from the sea. Maybe a seagull dropped it, or it fell from the case of someone back from holiday. You may not think that is magical, but a week later I was given a big conch shell made into a musical instrument. When you blow into it, it makes a deep booming sound, like waves hitting rocks. So the finding of the shell was a message that something bigger was on the way.

Fill your book with unusual events, sightings, thoughts, ideas and bits knowledge. This trains the mind, the eye and the magical senses to gather information that ordinary people never notice. You may find the same idea, symbol or piece of information coming up again and again. This means it is trying to tell you something, so look for an explanation. Take note of unusual happenings as they might be a sign of something on its way to you. If you keep finding bird feathers for instance, it could mean a letter, a journey, or news coming from far away. A rubber band holds things together, so it could mean a new, or an old friend coming to visit. In the next chapter, I will tell you about symbols and how to read them.

If you find a coin, keep it in a box until you find another and add them. Coins are meant to be together in order to become 'more'. They attract each other and, once you have two or three, they will call others to join them. Hold the thought of a certain amount, not a lot because that's greedy, say a pound, and when you get that *give it to someone who needs it*. Because what you give with a good heart and a blessing, will come back to you doubled.

Here are a few spells you can put into your magical diary.

A Feather Spell

This is a very old spell and dates from 1500.

Find a bird's feather and whisper a wish into it. On a windy day, toss it into the wind and chant:

Up a day, down a day,
High, high, high!
Let my wish go on its way,
Fly, fly, fly!
Find a smiling angel
In the sky, sky, sky.
Ask him if he'll make it true,
He'll ask why, why, why?
For it will make me dance and sing,
Sigh, sigh, sigh,
Witchlet come and dance with me
High, high, high,
And I will make your wish come true
Bye and bye and bye.

Stating Your Magical Name

When working a spell, you can include these lines. Always begin by saying your magical name.

I am ....!

Witches might and witches main
All are hidden in the name
Choose with care that it may be
A secret in the heart of thee.
Let it hold a meaning clear
Of all that's good within thee dear.
That you can say when day is done
I did my best and it harmed none.

Planting Spell

Gnomes of earth now gather round
And give a blessing to this ground.
Sweet and fresh this earth must be,
Fed with moon water as a fee.
Sow the seedlings small and frail,
Guard them from the hungry snail.
Each tiny shoot will blessed be,
Each flower a gift from me to thee.

Moon Spells

The moon holds a lot of power. After all, she can raise the oceans of the world twice a day. As the *New Moon* she makes things grow. As the *Half Moon* she gives special dreams. As the *Full Moon* she is most powerful with spells. As the *Dark Moon* she can take things away, like anger, bad dreams, hurts, and tears.

Dolores Ashcroft-Nowicki

New Moon Chant

When you see a new moon, bow to her nine times and whisper quietly:

Lady Moon, Lady Moon, shining up above,
Send to me a blessing and I'll send to you my love.
Help me grow up straight and strong and help me to be wise,
And I will bless you every month, my Lady of the skies.

Half Moon Chant

At the half moon, catch her image in a small mirror and repeat three times while looking at it:

Moon Mother, Moon Mother, a child of Earth am I.
Grant me dreams of joy and peace as on my bed I lie.
Moon Mother , Moon Mother hold me soft till dawn
And I will wake to face the day as if but newly born.

Full Moon Chant

At the full moon, gaze upon her and sway from side to side as if dancing. Repeat three times:

Moon Dancer, Moon Dancer, listen to my song.
Let us dance together, our steps both light and strong.
Let Apollo's music guide our steps this night,
And we will keep on dancing until the dawn's new light.

Apollo is the ancient Greek god of the sun.

Dark Moon Chant

At the dark of the moon, stand with arms crossed over your heart, while looking up at Her. Stand silent for a while then repeat with feeling:

Moon Mother, Moon Mother, listen to my plea,
There are things that trouble me, from which I would be free.
Moon Mother, Moon Mother, calm my fears I pray,
And give me strength to face my fears and see them pass away.

To Make Moon Water

Moon water was, and still is, used to wash your face and clear the skin, or to give a final rinse to your hair. It was also used when sowing seeds in spring. Give them a drink of moon water to make them grow strong. Elderflower soaked in moon water, and either drunk or used to make tea, was said to give strength and calm a fever.

Fill a shallow bowl with water from a flowing stream or river, then lay it out under the moon on the evening *before* she is full. Place the bowl carefully so that the moon's light falls directly onto the water. Move the bowl to keep the moon power filling it as she moves across the sky. Then cover it. Do this each night until the moon is past full, then bottle the water and use within seven days. A few drops in bath or shower is said to wash away any ill-wishing sent to you.

Look for moon lore that older family members might have to share with you and look in old books on traditional herb lore. In olden times, a bride always washed in moon water on her wedding day, and new-born babies were washed with it too.

Filling Your Magical Diary

The information in your magical diary will grow as you learn more. The more you know, the more you will understand the world about you and the world within you. Don't be afraid to ask for information. Many gardeners know a lot about moon lore, even if they are not in the Craft themselves. Reading is not the only way to learn. The more you seek, the more knowledge will be attracted to you. As you get older you might like to learn how to make oils and creams from herbs and flowers. Such a skill was highly prized in ancient times.

All these bits of knowledge should be written down in your magical diary by hand. This will make it more personal than recording it on a computer or an iPad. Electronic devices allow 'emotion' to 'leak' out and, as you will learn as you grow older, emotion is what magic is all about. The Craft has always been recorded by hand so that the power flows from you to the book and back again. Remember this – the book is as much a magical tool as your wand, cup, or robe, and should be used as such.

When you begin, this will all seem very exciting, but there will be a time when new ideas and new interests will take its place. This is natural, and it is all part of growing up. You may even find yourself putting the magical diary and other things aside. But, once you set foot on the path of magic, it will call you back when the time is right and when you are old enough to begin taking magic seriously.

There is a right time for everything, including school, learning to deal with world and the people in it. Even in this time you will find some who will see what you believe in and how you express your beliefs as wrong. As long as you keep to the witch's rule of *And It Harm None,* you are entitled to worship as you choose. Behind you lie thousands of years of ancient wisdom, and you are the heir to that wisdom.

Chapter Thirteen
The Inner and Outer World

There are many kinds of magic, and one often leads into another without you knowing. This is because, strange as it may seem, this whole universe is magical, it's just that few people realise it. Even simple things, like growing up, are magical. So sooner or later you will find your magical diary sitting patiently on a shelf, waiting for you to remember it. Meanwhile, another important part of you has been growing. So important that it is often seen as being a whole new world, one that lives inside your head. We call it *imagination*.

The *inner world* is as real as the *outer* one, just different. Witches and pagan people accept that they can visit the inner world and meet and work with those who live there. Your inner world also needs attention, so you should set aside time to visit and get to know and use it. You will make friends there who will always be happy to see you. But the outer world is where your everyday life is spent; where you will grow up and one day have a family of your own. So, learn to tell the difference and, though they can help each other, they must never be allowed to affect each other too much.

The outer world is *real* and demands effort from you. The inner world is gentler and can sometimes be so beautiful you want to stay there, but it has its own dangers. If too much time is spent there, you can become dreamier and less able to deal with the real world. *But you must not allow that to happen.* Occasionally, people forget there is a real world and try to stay in the inner world – then find they cannot get back. Put this in your Magical Diary and *underline* it.

The Gate to the Inner World

Imagine a high wall of coloured bricks with a door, or gate set into it. Instead of a lock, put the palm of your hand against the door, close your eyes and imagine that it makes an imprint on the door that will remain there and act as a key. The only way into your inner world will be by placing your hand on that palm print. Speak your name, then say a special word that *you have chosen* to open it. Then, and only then, can you enter, and it will close behind you. Never give that word to anyone else.

To close the gate when you leave, place your hand on the print and *spell out the opening word backwards.*

Remember what I have told you; in magic, *intent* holds power. Your intent is to open and close the door to your inner world, so the door will obey you. This means that when you leave, you become aware of being in the real world again. It may seem a silly thing to do, but it is important and will become something you do without thinking after a while. You need to know the difference between the two worlds and *feel* the difference in yourself.

It is a precaution so that you never get locked into the inner world.

Another word of warning: There is a very old belief that when you are in the inner world, you *never* eat or drink anything offered to you, even if you see something you like – fruit on a tree or water from a stream. The belief is that if you do, you can never leave.

You might like to visit the library and read a poem by Christina Rosetti called *Goblin Market*, as this gives an example the dangers I describe above.

Chapter Fourteen
The Full Moons of the Year

As you get older and begin to read more about pagan ways, (and I hope you will, because they are interesting to read and beautiful to be a part of), you will find that a lot of it is bound up with the Moon and Sun and with lunar and solar cycles.

In the beginning of human evolution, the Sun was the first and most important *God* to the people. It gave warmth and light to the world around them. It appeared every morning but disappeared at night, causing fear and danger to everyone. Animals with night sight went on the prowl then, hunting for food both four-legged and two-legged. So, the Sun's return was looked for eagerly, and it was the first object to be worshipped as a god. When the Sun set each night, there was something else to replace its light. This orb was smaller; it had no warmth and its light was not as strong, but it was enough to give a feeling of safety through the long hours of darkness. This was the Moon.

The Sun was seen as being like the tribe's hunters; big, strong, fierce, and able to protect. So, it was seen to be male, and all the hunters tried to be the same. But the Moon was smaller, softer and gentler. It was seen as being a comfort during the night, when loud noises and strange creatures made everyone huddle together. It made the young ones seek their mother's warmth. So, the Moon became seen as *motherly* and female.

Later still, because women were the ones who gathered edible roots, fruit, berries and wild grains and knew where to find them, they and the moon became linked to the Earth and the power of being able to grow things, including children. Women were the ones who kept the tribal family together, so the Moon, the Earth, and the loving Mother became a triple goddess, seen as the Sun's equal, and in some cases, the primal or first creator of all life.

While the Sun was always the same shape, the Moon went through a series of changes; from the *Crescent New Moon*, to the *First Quarter*, then the *Half Moon* and *Full Moon*, and finally to the *Dark Moon*. When she was dark, and the Sun went down, it was a time when there seemed to be no light in the world at all, so people began to think of the dark Moon as being a time when the Great Mother had deserted them, and bad things happened. So, the dark of the Moon began to be seen as a time of evil. But *time* itself is like *space*, neither evil nor good: it just is.

This is a good time to tell you that, although people talk about black magic, in actual fact there is no such thing –

magic is just magic, as time is just time. *It is the use to which magic is put* and, most important of all, the kind of people who use it, that makes it good magic or bad magic.

Remember what I taught you at the very beginning? '...and it harm none.'

Without watches or clocks, the witches and pagans of early times looked to the heavens for guidance, both seasonal and daily. You got up with the Sun and went to bed when it went down – at least until we learned to use fire to provide extra light. At night, though, they had the Moon. It has a regular twenty-eight-day cycle with a *face* that changes shape each seven days. This was enough to tell them how much time had gone by and how long it took to do or make something. They named each full Moon in turn, according to the work that needed to be done, or the time of year.

The community in which I was taught also named the Dark Moons. But, in the early days, the names changed from tribe to tribe, and in the Middle Ages, when many isolated and rural communities were mostly pagan, they often changed from village to village. The ones I am going to give you are the names that were given to me, but understand they are not the only ones, and you may hear or read about others.

In those days all villages had a *village green*. This was an area of grass, surrounded by cottages, small houses, and often a bakery. It usually had a central area where a fire pit lined with brick was dug. Most houses would have a small front garden with a wooden gate. On the gate might be a sign showing a symbol of some kind. A needle and thread with a pair of shears meant a seamstress was available for work. A loom shuttle meant a weaver.

Crossed quill pens stood for someone who could read and write. An old leather shoe meant a shoemaker, and a chisel or hammer and nail was a carpenter. The village green was also a meeting place and many of the community's ceremonies were held or begun there.

January Moon
Snow Moon

January was a time when the most isolated villages were snowbound until the thaw. There were, however, still traditions and ceremonies that were celebrated no matter how bad the weather. On a chosen day in the New Year, all the house fires in the village were put out. The only one spared was the forge fire that belonged to the blacksmith, which was kept lit continuously. The village *Master of Ceremonies*, usually referred to as *The Dancer*, lit a *bonefire* on the village green, and the men folk gathered around in a circle, hands on each other's shoulders. Herbs were thrown onto the fire to make it smell sweet and, at the Dancer's signal, the men would begin to circle the fire and chant:

Hail the fire, the leaping flame,
See it dancing, ne'er the same.
Hand in hand we circle round,
What was lost can now be found.
Quick and quicker dance the feet.
Fast and faster the heart doth beat.
Hand in hand we circle round,
By the flame we all are bound.
Hail the fire, Hail the fire, Hail the fire.

This was repeated several times until the Dancer raised his staff. He passed round a horn cup filled with ale, from which they all drank. Then each man took a burning brand from the fire and ran home with it to light the New Yarl Fire. In some areas, a coin was placed in each man's shoe, so that he could walk wealth into his house. (The word yarl is an old north country name for year.)

February Moon
Death Moon

This was a time when the young and elderly were at increased risk of illness. Until the coming of modern medicine, it was expected that during this moon there would be losses in the family. On Candlemas, which was celebrated on 2nd February, the front step of each house was washed in wine or ale and whitened with a special stone. Often, the boundaries of the village would be walked in procession and the boundary stones anointed with milk and honey to keep evil at bay. In this month, knives, axes, plough shares and anything with a blade was sharpened ready for the spring. The *Tallow Maid* ritual was also celebrated on this moon. (See the last chapter.)

March Moon
The *New Leaf* or *Greening Moon*

Sowing the land for the new harvest was now in full swing. The ploughs were out in many places, but in the north of England, where the ground would still be partly frozen, the ceremony of the *First Furrow* took place in early March. For this, the Shire horses were decked with bronze medallions, their tails braided, and harnesses polished. The honour of *First Furrowing* was much sought after, and everyone gathered at the chosen field. A new-laid egg was placed halfway down the field to be cut into the earth by the plough as an offering to the Earth Mother, asking for her blessing. It was a festival when young men and boys tried their hand at cutting a straight furrow, with a prize for the best. Housewives planted their herb gardens and fields that had lain fallow were sown with seed blessed by the village. Winter clothing, blankets and linens were washed, dried in the March winds, then packed away. The making of the *Green Witch* was also celebrated on this moon. (See the last chapter.)

April Moon
Green Moon or *Maiden's Moon*

In ancient times, on the last day of this month in villages all over Britain, the *Beltane Maid* and her partner the *Horned Lord* were chosen from the community. They represented the god and goddess of nature. The *Rite of Beltane* was celebrated on *May Eve* (30th April) and went on through the night into the first of May. Everyone wore something green, either as clothing or a ribbon in their hair. The celebration went on all through the night. Part of this month's moon festivities were the *Raising of the Green Man*, another aspect of the growing season. This too was celebrated with song and dance

May Moon
The *Courting Moon*

On the first day of May, it was time to raise the Maypole on the village green. Taken from its winter store and the covers removed, it was washed, oiled, dressed with new ribbons, and carried through the village on the shoulders of the young men. Then it was raised, with a lot of hurrahs, on the green. It stood for seven days and dancing took place every day during that time. The first to dance were the *Beltane Maid* and her *Horned Lord* together with their chosen friends. In the mornings and afternoons, the children had their turn. Later in the day and in the evenings, the young men came with their girlfriends and danced, while the old folk sat and gossiped about their youth. It was a time when friendship grew into something deeper, which is why it was called the *Courting Moon*.

June Moon
Rose or *Wedding Moon*

Halfway through the year – and life was easier. Crops grew tall, farm animals had had their young, and the days were long and warm. There was still work to be done, but there was also time for fun, games and weddings. *Hare and Hounds* was a game for the young men: The 'hare' was chosen and given a head start, usually half an hour. It was his task to stay ahead of the 'hounds' and to arrive back at the green by a certain time. A skilled hare, who knew the area well, could and often did, lead the hounds all over the countryside for hours. They might get back tired, hungry and thirsty to find the 'hare' sitting in the inn, drinking cider. There was another version of this later in the year, but it was run with a different purpose.

This full Moon was the *Day of the Dancer*, the village 'wise man'. He was honoured for his power and his work through the year. He was given food, ale, clothing and other gifts by the villagers. His tradition is pre-Saxon, and would take too long to describe here, but he was an important part of village life, though he was sometimes known by different names, for over a thousand years, in Britain.

July Moon
Lightning Moon

This was almost a holiday month. Summer storms could – and did – flatten whole fields of corn. After all, it is St

Swithin's month (his festival took place on 14th July.) Tradition says that if it rains on St Swithin's Day, it will rain for forty days! However, it is a time for farm work to ease up a little. Time to weed the garden and reshoe the horses. The women would spend time sewing, knitting, spinning and weaving. Meanwhile, the menfolk repaired things, carved wooden toys and got under everyone's feet. This full Moon was celebrated by *The Goodwives*. It was the custom for a husband to give a little bell (a miniature wedding bell) to his wife. She would hang it on a hook next to the hearth fire. You could tell how long she had been married by counting the bells. This was also a time for children to gather round the elders of their communities and learn the old songs, dances and folklore.

August Moon
Lammas Moon

This was a sort of early harvest festival. The first day of August was *Lammas* time and was a special day in ancient Britain. The word *Lammas* comes from the old Saxon *hlâf–Maesse* meaning Loaf Ritual or Loaf Mass. A special bread was made from the first batch of ripe corn ground into flour and was shared by all. Eating just a few crumbs was thought to bring good health through the year.

It was the custom in the early days to offer a sacrifice at this time. This follows the custom of sacrificing the *Corn King* that goes back beyond ancient Egypt. In many areas, being made a 'king' often meant you might reign for certain length of time, after which you 'died' for the good of your people, and became a power in another dimension, like 'heaven'. To offer the life of the Corn King was thought to make sure the next harvest would be a good one.

Remember this, it is important: Traditional celebrations in very ancient times were thought to hold a lot of power over people's lives. Life was much harder then, harder than we can imagine today. This meant that some of the old celebrations contained actions that today we would find horrible, and very wrong. But in those days, they were seen as necessary for the good of the community.

Things are no longer the same, and such sacrifices are not necessary, but the *idea* of celebrating the *First Loaf* is still used. Making bread is very magical, as it involves the four elements: Flour (grain) from the *Earth* is the basic ingredient, then *Water* is added to make the dough. When you knead the dough, you force *Air* into it as you do so, and then you bake the loaf in a hot oven using *Fire*. Bread has always been one of the most basic human foods and, in various ways, it is made and used daily by almost every person in the world.

September Moon
Falling Leaf Moon

This is the main harvest festival of the year. Churches and other organisations celebrate it as a time of giving to those who do not have enough. It is a sacrifice of a different nature, for we give what we have to those in need, and we do it without taking life. In many pagan groups, it is a time to gather and dry herbs, make jams from the fruits, cut and dry apples and store them. In short, we prepare as humans have always done, for the coming winter. In places where snow is a problem, we store candles, batteries for torches, and tinned foods. We have means to preserve food stuffs more easily now. In the north of Britain there are many deep caves where, in times gone by, meat was salted and hung up high, where animals couldn't reach it, but it was cold enough for ice to keep the meat fresh. On this moon, pagans gathered to *Bed the Green Man Down* with song and dance.

October Moon
Hunter's Moon

This was the time to cull the deer herds; choosing the older stags and those unlikely to survive the winter. Partridges, pheasants, rabbits and hares were all food sources and were hunted, though care was taken not to take too many. This moon celebrated the coming of *Herne the Hunter* and his *Wild Hunters*, and also the *Great Gathering*. In a time when it was dangerous to be a pagan or witch, the coming together of a large gathering was rare, and happened maybe once or twice in ten years, but everyone tried to attend at least two or three times in their life. News of families, births and deaths were shared and often, as was the custom in those days, marriages were arranged.

The meeting place changed each time. Wild moorlands with high hills were ideal sites, so that strangers could be seen easily by the look-outs and word spread so that people could disappear into caves, woodland, and farmland. The meeting lasted for two or three days and nights, and a bonefire was lit on top of the hill with cooking fires below. The first to arrive were the 'wise people' of the community to make sure all was prepared. Others arrived in small groups, coming from all directions. Villagers offered the shelter of their homes, barns and even stables. The host village supplied the *Herne*, the *Horned Lord of the Wild Hunt* (its Nordic name was the *Einherjar* – say it as *ain-hare-yah*.) The visitors offered their strongest men to be the huntsmen. You will find one of the legends of the wild hunt in the last chapter of the book.

The last evening of the month was the celebration of All Hallows, when the dead were allowed to come close to the living. There are many ways of celebrating this time, and different communities have their own way of doing so. It has become more of a precursor to Christmas. Children dress up as witches, ghosts and vampires and go from house to house collecting gifts of sweets and money. The old ritual calling of the dead has now almost been lost.

However, it is still the custom in some areas for families to put together a simple meal and gather at family gravesides to eat and drink with the dead. It may sound a little gruesome, but it is more like a party, and lets the dead – the ancestors – know they are still part of the family. I have seen this done in Philadelphia and also in Mexico, where this day is a full-on festival, with music, dancing, costumes and lots of food and drink. In Britain it is a lot quieter, although children take part in the practice of Trick or Treat, even if some frown upon it.

November Moon
Long Knife Moon

This was a sad time, for not all the cattle, pigs, geese and other animals could be kept through the harsh winter. But in the community where I learned my craft, their death was quick and done with a blessing as a gift for what they would provide as sustenance. They were usually washed and given special food for a few days beforehand, and some families even spent the night before with their animals. In the old days, the meat was salted and hung in the caves, but in the late 70s several of the larger farms had freezer units and shared them with their neighbours. When hunting, there was an unwritten law that set a limit on how much a hunter could 'bag'. As good pagan folk they were aware that if you killed too many, you would lose them all eventually. This moon also celebrated Anvil Day. The local blacksmith would place gun powder under his anvil and set it off with a charge. This lifted the anvil into the air often by several feet. 24th November is St Clement's day; the patron saint of blacksmiths.

December Moon
Old Yarl's Moon

Christmas, Mabon, New Year or Yarl – so many festivals going on and all of them mixing religions, pagan practices and folklore. This is the time when the year pivots, and we all look back at what has happened, and then look forward to the coming year with hope. You, the children I hope will be reading this, are a living part of that hope. As pagans, you are like lanterns, for you are the ones who will carry the light of the old ways into the future.

Some of the things we have shared will seem old-fashioned, but there is a strength in them that has kept them alive for thousands of years. Remember everything has to have a foundation; a basis on which to build. To have a belief in something bigger and stronger than yourself, and with the feel of mystery about it, is to have a *faith* all of your own. It is children like you, and you, and you, who have kept the pagan ways alive over the centuries. It is because children have remembered them and passed them to their children that we still have a belief in *real magic*. Not the magic of Disneyworld, but the magic of knowing there is always something to find, explore, believe in, talk about and share. This book was written so I could tell you how important *you* are, because you are our future.

Chapter Fifteen
The Magical Language of Symbols

Symbols are the oldest form of communication, possibly even before real speech. It might have happened because someone found they could make a mark on a cave wall with a bit of burnt stick. From then on, it was established as a way of letting those behind you know which path to follow.

Pedlars, gypsies, and travellers have their own signs and symbols that tell those following them if a certain house has dogs, will be friendly or not, or can be asked for water, or old clothing. Soldiers have a system of hand signals that show when to stop, carry on, spread out, or take cover.

I am sure that you have, or will soon have, a mobile phone, and though they are useful, and at times life-saving, they are also destroying the art of writing.

Because, with mobile phones, we often use symbols to convey meaning in the shortest possible way.

For example: *RUOK?* is a series of symbols that replaces everyday words, but it is understandable instantly as a question on a mobile. *CU2MRO* translates as *see you tomorrow.* So, in many ways, we have gone back in time and communicate like our ancestors in symbols instead of writing (which takes longer.) But symbols can hold a lot of meaning once you know how to read them. The secret lies in looking at their various parts.

One of the best-known symbols is called an *ankh* and is most often seen in ancient Egyptian pictures. But the ankh is now easily recognised and often used in Western magic and pagan rituals. Its basic meaning is *life* and it is usually carried or held by Egyptian gods as a symbol of their immortality. It can have other meanings too, if you look at how it is made up:

First there is a *circle or loop* – this can be a symbol of the sun or it may mean daytime, creation, light, warmth or growth. All things that the sun provides.

——————— If you put the cross bar under the circle, it can mean the horizon, a balance, a division of time or space, or simply a resting space. It represents support, strength, something to lean on – like a stick when you are tired. All in all, when put together, these three symbols signify a 'a length of time, a balance of energies, both physical and mental, and a strong support' – all things we need to ensure a long and healthy life.

Sun on the horizon is a way of saying dawn, sunset, or a

day in time. Put the support under the circle and cross bar and it can mean life is beginning, or something new will happen. It can also mean healing, as it uplifts the sun and makes it strong.

Interpreting Symbols

In ancient times, there were no linking words – no ifs, ands, or buts. You had to make a guess at the meaning by looking at the whole sentence. Now you can see why *scribes* were very important people.

Of course, there are many more symbols than these, all from different countries. The First Nation people of America did not develop writing but, like the Egyptians, they used a combination of glyphs and hand signals. Their spoken languages were well adapted to their ancestral surroundings and were very expressive.

The Eye in a Triangle

This is seen on the American dollar bill. It symbolises, among other things, the eye of the creative being watching over humankind, (presumably to see what we are doing.) We have a saying; 'I'll keep my eye on you.' It reminds us that even if we think no one can see us doing something wrong, it will be found out eventually and not always in the way we had hoped.

If you look at an American dollar bill you will find that it has many symbols and they all have a magical meaning. If you don't already know about them, ask someone who does. (Never be afraid to ask questions, that is how you learn.)

The Hand of Fatima

Again, this is an ancient symbol that is both protective, and healing. It is a feminine symbol, like the Great Mother looking after Her children. In Islam, Fatima was the name of Mohammed's wife, but that doesn't mean that it can't be used by other faiths. It is the way in which a symbol is used, and the quality of the power put into it, that matters.

The Pentagram

The pentagram, or 5-pointed star is often seen as something that is bad or evil by people who don't know its history. In actual fact it is one of the oldest symbols in the world and can be found in almost every tradition. Its true meaning, in the simplest form, is the coming together of the five elements: earth, water, fire, air and spirit. It can be used to bring them together within yourself, or over your altar. Don't be afraid to use the pentagram, for it symbolises the completeness of the elements within you.

The Swastika

Symbols can used for both good and bad purposes. The swastika is one of the oldest symbols in the world, used in several countries for thousands of years as a spiritual symbol. It originally meant prosperity, luck, the sun and divinity, among other positive meanings.

However, in magical work, if a symbol is used over a period of time to cause harm, it *goes bad*, like food kept for too long. It is gradually changed, in a way, so that the real meaning is hidden or forgotten, and a new, wrong meaning is associated with it instead.

 This is an ancient version of the swastika, or 'sun wheel' version, turning clockwise from left to right. It held the meaning of a new day and light.

Eighty years ago, a man who knew a lot about magic but used it to cause harm, saw a way to use this symbol to hurt. He changed its direction, so that it moved anti-clockwise. His actions plunged the world into war and millions of people died in terrible ways.

This is why, in the first chapter, I taught you the witch's rule – *'and it harm none.'*

Symbols are indications of thoughts, ideas, and intentions and can affect our emotions in many ways, which is why we rely on them to relay how we feel to those around us. Gesture is a part of this as well. We clap our hands to indicate pleasure. We offer an open hand to a stranger to indicate we have no weapon in it. We point a finger to indicate the location of something, or even to show displeasure. We open our arms to a loved one and embrace them – holding them close to our heart centre to share its life force with them. We kiss, pressing mouth to mouth and copying an age-old method of feeding a child. Many animals still do this.

Television adverts use symbols all the time. Because they are visually designed to make you *look, recognise, want,* and *buy.* The best adverts make you imagine yourself doing, eating, wearing or using that particular product. Once you understand that, you see that television adverts are like magical spells – they make you want what they are selling even if, when you get it, you wonder why you ever bought it.

See how many symbols you can find on your way to school – on traffic signs, on adverts, in shop windows, and on the sides of buses. When you get home, draw them, study them and work out what they are saying and how they might affect you.

Almost everything we do has grown out of ancient ways and carries traces of our past. Learning about symbols will increase your skill in understanding the people around you, because we signal our intentions ahead of time. You may not understand this now, but as you get older, you will be able to judge character by the words, gestures and habits of people around you. This will give you an advantage in life, in work, and in your dealings with others.

As you work with symbols, you many find one repeating itself in your life in a positive way, or affecting you by making you feel strong, lucky, happy or relaxed and aware of something about to happen. This becomes a personal signal from your inner powers; it can warn you of dangers or good fortune, or a need to take a certain action, by an increase in your psychic awareness. This can take time to become a real magical power, but it is a possibility.

We all have strong points and weak points in our magical selves and recognising them takes time. But starting young is a help. You will learn to put up with ridicule, and even real animosity, from disbelievers, but don't let it bother you. Do not let too many people know of your interest in magic. Keep your ideas to yourself, unless someone shows real interest, even then be aware they may have an ulterior motive. Magical people learn early how to protect themselves.

This is a short chapter because *you* must begin to do practical work now. Search for a symbol that interests you, draw it, colour it, not once but many times. Try different sizes, colours, forms, and put them where you can see them clearly. Put one under your pillow and sleep with it. Let it talk to you, tell you about itself and then write down what you learn. There is a time in learning when you have to stop reading and *do* something.

Don't use the first symbol you think of, but take your time choosing it. Don't hurry and, if possible, begin at the new moon so that your understanding of the symbol can grow with the moon's power, peak at full moon, then sink inwards as the moon wanes. There are places on the internet where you can find out about symbols and their meaning. You can also learn how to read and draw hieroglyphs and ancient alphabets.

Chapter Sixteen
Gods and Goddesses

Each tradition has its own collection of gods and goddesses called a *pantheon*. Pan is a Greek word meaning all and *Theon, or Theo,* means God or Divinity. There are usually twelve in a pantheon, though some traditions have more, and there are also types of divinities who have no specific power but are more like nature spirits.

Greek

Zeus is the High King and rules the air, thunder and lightning.

Hera is his wife and queen. She looks after the home and women in general, including marriage and children.

Hephaestus is the eldest son of Zeus and Hera. He rules

the art of the blacksmith and creates magical weapons like his father's lightning bolts and armour.

Ares is their younger son. He is the god of war, soldiers and battles.

Apollo is the God of the Sun and drives the Sun chariot across the sky each day. He is also a famous archer. He has a twin sister called Artemis.

Artemis is Apollo's twin sister. She drives the chariot of the Moon and is the goddess of hunting.

Hermes wears winged sandals and a winged hat and carries a staff topped with a pine cone. His staff also has twin snakes twined around it and two wings at the top. He is the messenger of the gods.

Aphrodite is the goddess of love and beauty.

Athene is the goddess of wisdom and knowledge. She carries an owl on her shoulder.

Demeter is the Earth goddess and looks after the growing things.

Hades is the brother of Zeus and rules the underworld. He has a three headed dog called Cerberus.

Poseidon is Zeus's third brother and he rules the oceans and rivers and causes earthquakes.

Roman

The Romans had the same gods as the Greeks did, who personified the same things, but they gave them different names:

Jupiter = Zeus
Juno = Hera
Mars = Ares
Helios = Apollo
Diana = Artemis
Mercury = Hermes
Minerva = Athene
Venus = Aphrodite
Ceres = Demeter
Pluto = Hades
Neptune = Poseidon
Vulcan = Hephaestus

You will find more names when you begin to read the Greek and Roman myths. Eos is the Dawn. Pan is the Goat-foot God who looks after the wild creatures. Thetis is a sea goddess. Nephele rules the clouds while Vesta looks after the Sacred Fire in the temples.

The Greek and Roman gods are fairly easy to remember, and their time is closer to ours, less than two thousand years ago.

Egypt

The Egyptian pantheon is much older and there are a lot more gods and goddesses within it. The Ancient Egyptian civilisation lasted nearly four thousand years, so they tended to change their gods and add new ones as they made contact with other lands and people

Their Creator God form was Atum or sometimes Atum Ra. Before him, there was Mut – the Unknowable or Chaos. Atum can be seen as the first member of a divine family of gods and goddesses. He created the twins Shu (god of dryness and air) and Tefnut (goddess of moisture and water). From these two came another set of twins – Nuit and Geb. Nuit was the stellar (star) goddess and her brother Geb ruled the Earth. They wanted to be together all the time, but Atum said they had to be apart. He told Shu (the air) to put himself between them, which was how the sky came to be raised above the earth. But Nuit was unhappy about this. Her tears became rain on the earth. In this way, the Egyptians explained earth, then air, the stars above, and the life-giving rain. But before they were separated, Nuit and Geb created two sets of twins: Isis and Osiris, and Nephthys and Set. Here is a list of them and what they symbolised:

Atum – the creator
Shu – god of air and dryness
Tefnut – goddess of moisture and water
Nuit – goddess of the stars
Geb – god of the earth
Osiris – god of fertility and the afterlife
Isis – goddess of magic, life, daytime and motherhood
Nephthys – goddess of magic and night-time
Set – god of storms and chaos

The children of Nuit and Geb were seen as the most important of the gods. But there were many others, who all had their own powers. Among them were falcon-headed warrior god Horus, (son of Isis and Osiris); jackal-headed Anubis, Guide of the Dead; ibis-headed Thoth, god of writing and magic. (An ibis is an Egyptian bird rather like a heron.) There were also Khnum the Potter God, who made bodies on his wheel and was also a healer; Sekhmet, the lioness-headed goddess, who was a war deity. Many of these gods wore animal heads as a symbol of their particular power. For a while, until you know a lot more about the different gods and goddesses, that is enough to remember.

Scandinavia

The Norse gods of Scandinavia are more warlike, but as the Scandinavian people lived in a harsh climate, this was linked to survival. Like gods and goddesses in other pantheons, the Norse gods and goddesses all had certain powers.

Ymir - the creator god who began all things.

Odin – king of the gods. He hung for nine days and nights on Yggdrasil, the World Tree, and gave up one eye in order to gain wisdom.

Frigga – queen of the gods, Odin's wife.

Thor – god of thunder, who had a magical hammer.

Baldur – god of light and purity who, like many other gods of 'light', died a magical death.

Tyr – god of war and heroic glory.

Loki – the trickster god.

Hel – queen of the underworld.

Heimdall – the guardian of Asgard, the home of the gods

Frey – god of fertility, wealth and peace. He had a magical ship called Skidbladnyr.

Freya – goddess of love, beauty and opulence.

The Celtic Gods

Each of the Celtic gods and goddesses had many names because they weren't just worshipped in England, but Ireland, Wales, Scotland, Brittany, Ancient Gaul, and reaching into Flanders and further away. So their names were changed in each area. But this list shows the most common names used for them.

Danu – the Celtic mother goddess

Arianrhod – the moon goddess.

Brigid – a fire goddess later made into Saint Bridget.

The Dagda – known as the 'Good God' – like a cross between Zeus and Hercules. The father god.

Epona – the horse goddess

Eru – goddess of the land.

Lugh – often called 'Lugh of the Silver Hand'. The god of light. (His festival Lughnasadh coincides with Lammas on 1st August.)

The Morrigan – a goddess associated with battle; she could be both nice and not nice at all.

Aengus – a young, handsome, and charming god of youth, beauty and poetry.

Belenus – the god of the sun. He was similar to the Greek Apollo, with a horse-drawn chariot.

Camulus - sometimes known as Taranis, he was a god of war.

Cernunnos – similar to the Greek god Pan, the horned Cernunnos was horned the Lord of the Forests and Wildlife.

Andraste – a war goddess but probably of a localised tribe known as the Iceni, who were ruled by Queen Boadicea (also known as Boudicca).

Cerridwen – she is also recognised as being an important part of Celtic myth and legend, but more as part of the Welsh pantheon, along with Gwion, Mannanan the Sea God, Bran the Blessed, Rhiannon – a moon goddess – and many others.

All gods and goddesses are brought into being by humanity's need for guidance, protection and knowledge. Their powers are the same powers that exist within us, you and me, but we are still learning to develop and use them in the right way, which is why books like this are written.

So, myths are stories about the gods and how they used their powers. In the early days of humankind, it was believed that the gods walked the earth and spoke with men and women and that they even had children with them. The stories about them were meant to teach people how to live and behave. They all have something to tell us about life as it was lived then.

In Greek myth, Narcissus was a very handsome young man, and he was so proud of his good looks that he fell in love with his own reflection. As he looked at himself in the water of a deep pool, he bent over to kiss his other self, fell in and drowned. The teaching here is that vanity can be dangerous.

Another story tells us that one day Zeus and Hermes were walking on the Earth. It was very hot, and they were thirsty and hungry. Nearby was a cottage where an elderly couple lived who loved each other very much but lived in fear that if one of them died, the other would be left alone and helpless.

Zeus and Hermes asked if they might have water and something to eat. The couple were so poor they had little to offer but, because they were entertaining gods, they killed their only chicken and offered the last cup of milk from their goat. Zeus was so touched by their selflessness, and their love for each other, that he offered them a wish. They wished that they could die together and not be separated, so Zeus changed them into two beautiful trees growing so close that their branches entwined forever. That story tells us that generosity will always be rewarded.

Pagan people have their own symbolic images that represent seasons and magical people. In English folklore,

Herne the Hunter leads the Wild Hunt – warriors who can be called on for protection and help. Herne wears stag horns and so does his horse. He is a very ancient pagan god form and is sometimes called *Cernunnos*. The Beltane Maid is his bride, who he visits once a year on the Eve of May. Herne and his warriors may look fierce, but they are also helpful, and they protect both humans and the wild ones.

The Moon Mother goes through four changes each month: she is the Maid at the new Moon, the Bride at the first quarter, the Mother at the Full Moon and the Crone at the last Quarter. Some witches adjust their magical work to fit in with her power as it grows to full and then declines. All this is part of growing up in the pagan way.

When you are older, I hope you will read books by Joseph Campbell. He gathered myths from all over the world to show how they all talked about the same things, in the same kind of stories. He believed every tradition had a variation of *The Quest*, with the same purpose of teaching people how to live and behave towards each other.

Fairy tales, (which are not always about fairies), also show how things happen when you act in a certain way. Again, when you are older, you may read *Grimm's Fairy Tales*. But you have to be old enough not to be scared by them, because they can be frightening.

In the days when only a few people could read and write, storytelling was the only kind of schooling most people had. The art of telling stories was a very important way of letting people know what was going on in other parts of the country. Villages, and even towns, were so far apart that it was often a year or more before people knew they had a new king, or even that they were, or had been, at war. Myths, legends and fairy stories were the only means of spreading news and events and of teaching people about life and its problems.

In school, you might learn about the parables in the Bible. These tales were the equivalent of the myths and legends in the early traditions, but they came later. In earliest times, people living in small villages had no way of knowing about new ideas and ways of living, but if they heard a story, the meaning behind the story would slowly sink in, especially if it was repeated again and again.

You, living in the 21st century, can read a book, watch television, and understand what a newspaper is saying. Two to three hundred years ago you would not have been able to read or write if you lived far from a town. So you would have relied on people from another town or village to let you know what was happening elsewhere.

Chapter Seventeen
Four Moon Rituals for Beginners

Spells and rituals do not have to be long and complicated. Short, simple and direct ones like the following examples will always get good results.

New Moon

For this you will need: Fresh earth in a small pot, some herb seeds (lemon balm, dill, borage – any will do), a small cup of water and a small silver coin.

The new moon symbolises growth. The herb seeds represent you, since you are still growing. The coin (silver is the moon's colour) symbolises luck. This ritual is to bring good luck for the coming month.

Place the coin in the bottom of the pot and fill it with fresh earth. Wait until the New Moon is high in the night sky, then place your right hand over your heart and make nine slow bows of the head towards her.

Maiden Moon, Maiden Moon,
This night I ask a special Boon.
Three times Three I bow to thee
And offer silver as a fee.
May this time as fruitful be,
As seeds I sow to honour thee.
Silver Lady shining bright,
Grant the wish I make tonight.
May I grow both strong and true
To be a shining light like you.

Sprinkle the seeds on the earth and cover them with a little more. Gently drip the water over the seeds and hold the pot up to the moon for a few minutes. Place it in the moonlight, and again make a bow, three times three, and walk backwards out of the moonlight. (Try never to turn your back on the moon.)

Tend the herbs and use them when they are fully grown.

Half Moon

Half moon magic and spells strengthen something already begun. This could be a spell, a project, or a non-magical task of some kind. This is best done, if possible, by a pool, stream or river. It could be performed on a beach when the tide is coming in but take care not to be surrounded by the tide or cut off from land. (Undines don't understand that humans can be hurt by strong tides.)

If nowhere like this is available, fill a basin with water and add a drop of salt. Cut three hairs from your head and then cut the three hairs into nine pieces and cast them into the water as you invoke the Lady Moon, now half way through her cycle.

Lady Moon silver bright,
Lighting up the starry night,
May the task that was begun,
Continue now until it's done.
May all be well, complete and true,
I offer this my work to you.
Grant hands and heart and judgement be
All that is the best in me.
Like you, let Light within me shine
And blessed be both me and mine.

Offer up the bowl and the hair, turn three times and bow to her, then repeat twice more. Afterwards, go outside and empty the water and hair over the ground.

Full Moon

This is the fulfilled Mother Moon in all her power. It is right and proper at this time to honour her. If possible, dress in white but it is not obligatory. You will need some flower petals and wild flower seeds to scatter.

Mother Moon loves to see her children dance, and to dance under a full moon is to perform the oldest kind of worship. As you dance imagine your head, and heart and tummy button opening wide to drink in the moon's power. Let her fill you with her silver light, and with her dream power. You can play some music if you like, or sing, but above all dance. Move to a song and imagine her as a face looking down on you.

Moon Mother, Moon Mother, see me dance and sing.
Fill me with your radiance, as silver stars do ring.
My words of joy and love for you will fill the world with song
In and out and round about we'll dance the whole night long.

Ancient Mother, Queen of Tides, Goddess of the Night

Dolores Ashcroft-Nowicki

Hail Diana, Cybele, you are glorious in our sight.
Fill me with your magic power that one day I may be
A Server of the Ancient ways, as I say, so mote it be.

As you dance, scatter the flower petals and wild flower seeds. Bless the wild life around you and the growing things. Dance for as long as you feel able, then bow or curtsey to the Moon Mother and ask for her blessing and a special dream. Then go to bed and sleep deeply.

Dark Moon

Humanity has always been afraid of the dark. In prehistoric times things much bigger than humans came out at night and hunted them. Even today many people are afraid of the dark and think of it, and anything dark in colour, as evil. But good things grow in the dark; plants under the earth and beautiful crystals. Some animals live under the earth, and new babies grow in darkness, safe and warm inside their mothers. Moths come out at night as well, and some of them are as beautiful as the butterflies we see in the daytime.

We sleep and dream when it's dark and even the moon has to rest. Of course, that doesn't mean it goes out. But, magically, it's a time when the moon replaces the magical power she gave out during the month. We can help her to do that. Often, people do not understand that magical power works both ways. Gods and goddesses of all kinds, and from all traditions, need to rebuild their power. This was the idea behind sacrifices and offerings. When you make an offering, a part of your emotional energy goes with it. That energy is part of the universe and energy cannot be destroyed. So when we give something to someone with love, we also give part of our energy.

The dark moon is a time for going over what has been

done and said. Looking to see where we could have done better. Where we have done well, and not so well. It is not a ritual, but a time for thinking about things when we're alone. Try to set aside ten minutes every other day to think about your magical work.

Allow your thoughts to take you into the past and Grandmother Moon will weave teaching dreams for you. Try to have a small light in your room. If you are old enough to have a candle that is okay *but always ask your parents first if they give permission.* Better to have a small lamp that can be turned down to give a low light. Light is energy, which is why parties have a lot of light. But you want a dim light to allow your thoughts to take you from place to place inside your head. Don't lie on the bed, you will fall asleep. Sit up and put a cushion behind your back for support. Read the prayer slowly.

Imagine, inside your head, there is a whole magical world and you are standing before a silver door. It opens and you walk into a room filled with soft coloured lights. There are two chairs and in one of them sits an elderly lady in a black dress covered with stars. She has white hair and a warm smile. On her lap sits a white hare cleaning its whiskers. The Moon Mother loves hares; they are her special symbol.

Dark Moon Prayer

In the Dark of the Moon when all is still,
In dreams I stand on the top of a hill.
I see a castle and a welcoming light
That shines in the darkness against the night.
I know who it is that awaits me inside:
The one who controls the incoming tide.
The Moon has four faces she shows to me:
Maid, Wife and Mother and the oldest is She

189

Dolores Ashcroft-Nowicki

Who runs with the wolves and dances with hares,
Grandmother Moon, the Goddess who cares.
Welcome me, Lady, and show me the way
To recall the powers of the old Pagan Way.

Chapter Eighteen
Seasonal Rituals

This chapter, and indeed this whole book, is how I personally think about magic and working magic. It is important to understand that every book, lesson, idea, or teaching is coloured by what the writer, or teacher thinks or believes. This means sorting out which ideas *you* personally want to accept, believe, or follow. This book holds ideas, thoughts, rituals and lessons that I learned from my teachers *or found out for myself*. Whatever books you read, or lessons you attend, remember *you* always have the right make up your own mind what to believe in or accept. Part of it, all of it, or none of it. No teacher has the right to make you believe in something. They can only share what they know with you, then let you choose.

All the rituals in this chapter are short, but they are still effective.

Dolores Ashcroft-Nowicki

Springtime

Each season has purpose, power, a symbol, and a link to humanity. Spring's *purpose* is renewal, its *power* is growth, its *symbol* is the seedling and its *link to life* is *you*. Each day, week, month, and year you are renewed by the way you change in form and knowledge.

This is the time when the Earth wakes from its winter sleep and prepares to receive new life. Everything around us – fields, trees, animals and people – make ready to grow, change and become bigger, older, wiser, and more useful. It's the time when Herne the Hunter rides through the land with his warriors, blowing his great horn to awaken the Earth's powers and claim his bride.

Fields are ploughed and prepared for seeding. Animals welcome their new-borns. Days get longer, and snowdrifts melt into the earth to water newly-planted seeds. It's a time when you find you have outgrown shoes, and clothes, and everything is too small and too short. Last year's things are handed down to younger sisters and brothers, often causing quarrels and sulks.

Seed catalogues arrive, gardens are dug over and cattle are let out into the fields to graze. For pagans and those belonging to the Old Ways, it is a time of hope and gratitude at having made it through the winter months, and the seasonal rituals reflect this. Each year, a different field had the honour of being the first to be ploughed. The Blessing of the Earth was called *First Furrowing*, and young men held contests to see who could cut the straightest furrow with horse and plough. The winner had the honour of cutting the first furrow. A new-laid egg was laid in place and the plough had to cut into it and so bless the whole field by its sacrifice.

Spring Ritual

You will need: Two or three packets of herb seeds - dill, basil and parsley will do. Also, a bottle of water, a packet of salt, a trowel (or even a big serving spoon), an incense stick and matches, and a new-laid egg.

Find a private place in your garden, or a quiet corner in the countryside, or even in a window box will do. Remember, it is the intent that counts when working magic.

When you have found a place, mark it out with salt to set it apart. It need only to be about twelve inches square. Now dig it over, turning it so that the earth beneath shows a nice rich brown colour. Don't tread on it but take off your shoes and socks and stand facing north, which is the direction of the element of Earth.

Hold out your right arm and point your forefinger. Now draw a circle, in the earth, then point your finger into the centre of the circle and say:

I call upon Uriel, Archangel of the Power of Earth, to bless and make sacred this plot of earth, and the seeds that grow in it. My thanks and blessings to Mother Earth for Her Bounty.

Sprinkle salt over the earth.

I call upon Ghob, Elemental King of Earth, to bless this sacred space and the seeds sown into it.

Scatter the mixed seeds.

May they grow and give food and pleasure to the life of this place

Turn to the West, draw a circle and point into its centre, saying:

I call upon Gabriel, Archangel of the Power of Water, to bless and make sacred this plot of earth and the seeds that grow in it. Let rain fall soft on it and feed it with love.

Dolores Ashcroft-Nowicki

Sprinkle water over seeds.

I call upon Nixsa, the Elemental King of Water, to feed this plot of land with the Tears of Mother Earth, that they may grow and flower.

Turn to the South, draw a circle and point into its centre, saying:

I call upon Michael, Archangel of the Power of Fire, to bless and make sacred this plot of earth and the seeds that grow in it. May the warmth of the Sun give them strength and light to grow and give a Solar Blessing to the earth.

Light the incense stick and press it into the Earth.

I call upon Djinn, the Elemental King of Fire, to bless this sacred space and grant these seeds the gift of sunlight to aid their growth.

Turn to the East, draw a circle and point into its centre, saying:

I call upon Raphael Archangel of the Power of Air, to bless and make sacred this plot of earth and the seeds that grow in it. May the winds blow gently upon them and carry their scent over the earth.

Breathe over the seeds.

I call upon Paralda, Elemental King of Air, to bless this sacred space and the seeds sown into may they grow and give food and pleasure to the life of this place. I offer this gift of a new-laid egg to Mother Earth as she wakes from Her winter sleep. Welcome back to Earth.

Break the egg over the earth, then bury the shell pieces as well.

Summertime

Summer's *purpose* is increase, its *power* is vitality and its *symbol* is the hoe that keeps the weeds down. Its *link to human life* is joy, for this is a time when life is easier, and there is time to dance, play, and enjoy long days of warmth, and gentle evenings of companionship and story-telling. Fruit trees ripen, the corn fields turn to gold, and in ancient times, there would have been dancing on the village green. People could sit outside and drink home-made cider. There would have been games, like Hare and Hounds. It was time to make the *Green Witch*, which was a figure woven from willow branches, filled with goodies and tossed into the river as an offering to the Summer Queen. There were races to run, and new songs to be written and sung. Romany families travelled up from the south for the horse fairs, and talk turned to hopes of the harvest to come, and the great summer ritual of Lammas.

Summer Ritual for the Family

The Lammas ritual was, and in some areas still is, one of the biggest and most elaborate rituals of the year. The word Lammas comes from *'bread from the last sheaf, shared out.'* The power of the ritual is really an enactment of gathering the last sheaves and giving thanks for the bread that will be made from it. The actual Lammas King ritual is long and complicated, but for young witches like you I have made it quick and easy.

If you live near a cornfield that would be a really good place to go to do this ritual, but not everyone has one close by. However, you can buy bundles of dried corn in handicraft shops, and all you need is one or two bundles for decoration. It may be that one of your parents actually makes their own bread and can show you how to do it. If not, see if there is a real bakery near you who can make a special loaf for you and let you have fresh out of the oven. You can buy a ready-made loaf but *not* a sliced one. There are many kinds and shapes, but you need one that looks like this:

In Britain it is called a Cob loaf. Pop it in the oven for few minutes to warm it up. Then use the corn sheaves to decorate a wooden plate with the corn heads radiating out from the centre.

To begin the ritual, everyone gathers in the chosen place. Join hands and circle round singing the Lammas chant:

Lammas King, Oh Lammas King,
For thee we all now dance and sing.
By hoof and horn, by seed and corn,
We circle round this Lammas morn.

With joy we praise the Lammas King,
And as we dance and as we sing,
We call down blessings on his head,
For by his strength we will have bread.

His life he gives that we may fare,
Tho' now the field lies cold and bare.
The last sheaf makes the Lammas Cob,
And soup lies heating on the hob.
The Miller works within the mill,
But old and young will eat their fill.
The Lammas King within us lies,
We who live bless he who dies.

Lammas King, Oh Lammas King,
For thee we all now dance and sing,
By hoof and horn, by seed and corn,
We will feast this Lammas morn.

Circle three times, then the oldest person cuts the Lammas Cob and shares it round. The last crust is given to the birds or household pets, so they too can share its blessing.

Autumntime

Autumn can also be called Fall. This season's *purpose* is hope for a good harvest. Its *power* in ancient times was literally survival. Its *symbol* is the scythe with which the corn was cut. Now, we gather the harvest with tractors and combine harvesters, but long ago it was done by hand, so its *link to humanity* was the strength of the reapers as they swung the long-handled scythes from early morn to eventide.

In days gone by, a good harvest meant the survival of an entire village and a bad one could bring its death. In Britain, on Exmoor and Dartmoor in the south, and the northern moorlands in Yorkshire and Grindon, you can still find the remains of villages that failed to survive. A good harvest meant *life* in every meaning of that word. We still celebrate harvest festivals, in church services and in ritual. In Britain, churches collect food for the homeless and families in need, and pagan communities do the same. To give what can be spared, to go without, so that someone else can survive is the real power of autumn. In many ways it is a foretaste of the giving of gifts at Christmastide.

Autumn Rituals

There are three pagan festivals in autumn; Harvest

Festival, Halloween and the Feast of the Dead. In the United States, there's also Thanksgiving, which has its own celebration. Halloween is more of a children's festival now, but once it was a part of the Feast of the Dead and was celebrated by all faiths in their own ways. People still visit family graves, light candles and share picnics there. Mexico has a famous festival with costumes, music and street parties.

I am sure you have taken part in Halloween Trick or Treat parties and enjoyed them. So I have chosen a simple, more personal ritual for you to do. It is often forgotten that we mourn other deaths than those of family. The passing of a beloved pet also needs to be remembered. Their lives are shorter than ours, so it is likely that you have lost a pet or will in the future. They may be buried in the garden, or another favourite spot, so here is a short ritual for such a time and second one for the actual Harvest Festival itself.

Autumn Remembrance for a Beloved Pet

If you can go to the grave of your pet, perform the ritual there. If this isn't possible, find a special place outside, in your garden or somewhere similar.

Place a photo of your pet on its grave (or on the ground) and arrange a small candle and an incense stick before it. For a few minutes, recall a memory of your time together. Now light the candle and the incense, and then repeat the memory spell slowly, and with love.

You gave me love and now I see
How precious was that gift to me.
Your life was short but memory
Will always bring you back to be
The loved companion I once knew,
Please welcome me when life is through.

Giving Thanks for the Harvest

Giving thanks for a rich harvest in the autumn is a time-honoured rite. It can be celebrated in many ways, but I came across one way that seems both unusual and effective. Most places of worship hold a special service where food and gifts are collected and then given to those in need. But ritual does not always mean a way to give thanks. This is another way that you can do that, no matter how young you are.

Look for someone in need of help; perhaps an elderly neighbour or relative needs a bit of shopping, a garden cleared and weeded, letters to be posted or medicine to be collected. Simple things that take just a short time, which they cannot do for themselves. But always make sure your parents know them, and you have their permission to do this. *Do not* make this offer if you do not know the person concerned.

The pagan way of living includes community and offering help to others is a way of giving thanks for your own health, strength and mobility. If you know someone in need of this kind of help maybe you could offer just an *hour* of your time, once a week, to someone in need. It might be just to visit and talk, to shop, to write a letter and post it, to hang out some washing or collect a prescription. Older people need to talk about their memories, as it brings back their loved ones and their young days. They can tell you about history in a way that teachers can't do, because it *actually happened to them.*

This is not what you would call *magic* in the ritual sense, but it is a *gift* worth more than gold to the one receiving it. Make sure you know when they celebrate their birthday – your card (especially if handmade) may be the only one they will get. Bringing happiness, ending loneliness, giving someone an hour of your time, is a magical act of incredible power.

During the Second World War, my family and I were refugees from the Channel Islands, which were taken over by the Germans. My father was earning very little money and he was upset because he could not even afford to buy me a birthday card. But he made a cheque book out of an old note pad. Each cheque gave me *one whole hour* of his time. For each hour, I could decide what to do – maybe we'd visit a museum, take a long walk by the river Dee, or sit and talk so that he could answer my questions (and I always had questions.) He gave me his *time* and *attention*. Literally a whole hour of his life was mine. It was, and will always be, the most important and valuable present I was ever given. If you can offer that to someone, you will offer more than you know, for it is part of your own lifetime.

Wintertime

Winter's *purpose* is rest and recuperation for the Earth and all its life forms. Its *power* is inner silence and its *symbol* is a lighted candle in the window. This is the completion of a year of effort, hard work, learning new things, growing older and wiser, and survival. Its *link to life* is to be still, be quiet, take a deep breath, and think about what has been learned and endured.

The symbol of the candle in the window is an acceptance of what has been learned, *(enlightenment - look it up in the dictionary)*, and a sign to those still searching that there is a welcome waiting for them. Winter is seen as being dreary, cold, wet, and dark. But it's also a time of hot chocolate, roasted chestnuts, building snowmen and watching ghost stories on television. Families gather around a log fire and we celebrate Christmas. Its link is the togetherness of family, and a time to think of those who have no family, or home, fire, food and love. That is what the candle is for – to bring home those who may have lost their way.

Winter Ritual

Sometimes a ritual is nothing like what you might expect a ritual to be. It is an offering – a small sacrifice – something given to surprise someone who has no idea why they were chosen. Again, this is a simple act, but it may change someone's life. You should begin to plan it in early December, though it is actually done on New Year's Eve.

Begin to take notice of the people who serve you in shops, or cafes, on buses, and in post offices. Also, those who serve in other ways – postmen and women, delivery people, receptionists, counter staff in malls, shops, and markets. People you never really notice, but who provide a service for which they are seldom, if ever, noticed or even thanked. Take note if they smile, offer help, take time with you, do their work, even though they have been on their feet all day. Does anyone ever say *thank you* or tell them how helpful they have been?

Spend time making notes of those who do their dull jobs with a good heart. Choose three people who show this kind of quality. Then buy, or make, a small present. Something simple like a bunch of flowers, a pot plant, a picture in a frame from a charity shop, a book, pocket diary or a calendar. Wrap it up and write a card saying:

I want you to know how much your smile and your service mean to everyone around you. Even when you are tired, you take time to be helpful. I wanted to thank you and wish you a Happy New Year.

Surprise the person with the gift and tell them how you noticed them doing their work well and wanted to thank them. This gives them an energy boost and makes them aware of you as a special person. Ritual not only means something done in a temple, church or other special place. It means something done repeatedly. Until it becomes a habit. My grandmother always went back to try the lock on the front door. She knew it was locked, but unless she went back and made sure, she worried in case the door was open. It was a ritual for her.

Giving gifts at Christmas goes back further than the Three Kings bringing gifts to the baby Jesus in Bethlehem. It is the modern equivalent of making an offering to the gods. Basically, an offering is an exchange of energy. The universe is made up of energies of different kinds and strengths. We exchange energy when we shake hands, give a high five or a kiss, and when you *give,* you also *receive.*

Ritual is a way of offering energy to something very powerful. What you receive in turn from that something, is a much higher kind of energy. Which is why we feel so good after a ritual and usually have some kind of party or celebration. Universal energy keeps going round, and we get back as much as we give. You give a smile and a thank you; you get good service back. *Magic is a form of energy* and the more you share it, the more you get back. It can take many forms, but it remains an energy. A witch can spend a lifetime learning how to use it well.

Epilogue
So, What is a Witch?

A witch is someone who cares about the world we live in, and the life forms we share it with, whether they are mineral, vegetable or animal. They are someone who looks to the future, but also looks back to the strength and wisdom of the past. Someone who accepts other traditions and religions have a right to their beliefs but believes that they themselves are entitled to that same right. Witches respect the *sacred ground* of other faiths, be it a mosque, a synagogue, a cathedral, a Quakers' meeting house or a Buddhist temple. Honouring the faith of others honours the faith in your own heart.

Remember the *way of the pagan* is still regarded with suspicion by people of some other faiths. Be prepared for this to be a problem. Don't speak of your beliefs too openly or invite confrontation. Behave with dignity and keep emotions in check. As a pagan you belong to the oldest belief system in the world. Like all traditions, it had its dark times, but they are no longer part of the true pagan way.

Obey the laws of the land. Keep mind and body free of things that can harm you. Never lose a chance to learn something new, or to share knowledge with someone who is interested. Revere the Earth and Her younger children: without Her and them, you would not be here.

You are the future. You will be Earth's ambassadors, who will take humanity into space and meet with life in many forms. Take your beliefs with you and share them, but don't force them on others. You will encounter many beliefs different to ours, for *life* will always need something greater than itself to believe in.

The blessings of the ancient ones go with you.

About the Author

Dolores Ashcroft-Nowicki was born on 11th June 1929, on Jersey, the largest of the Channel Islands, where she spent her early childhood. She spent the war years as a refugee in the UK, but her family were able to return to Jersey after the war. Her paternal grandmother was in the Craft and had Romany blood, well mixed with some Spanish and German Jew and a spot of Scottish. Both her parents, Leslie and Jessica Ashcroft, were initiates. On the maternal side, her lineage is mainly North Welsh Druidic with craft in the mix. Her maternal grandfather was a member of the Golden Dawn magical order. So Dolores was brought up to work with magic on both sides of the family. In her teens she trained at RADA, then with LAMDA, and finally with Trinity College of Music. She gave up theatre when she married.

Dolores joined the Society of the Inner Light (Dion Fortune's School) in 1964 and took initiation in 1968. She later worked and trained with the well known and highly-respected author W.E Butler, and with him was a founder member of the internationally-known 'Servants of the Light School of Occult Science'. Dolores and Gareth Knight are now the only members left from those golden years, when the occult was making its way back into the public eye.

For ten years Butler trained Dolores as a Cosmic Meditator and finally passed the directorship of the school to her in 1976. For almost 50 years she guided the school, making it known and respected worldwide. She retired as Director in June 2018 but has not stopped working. She has over 30 books and two specially-designed Tarot decks to her credit and has lectured all over the world. She is known for her ability to share her knowledge and skill with laughter and a down to earth sense of fun. Her lectures are well-known for being filled with stories and anecdotes. Her whole life has been dedicated to making 'magic' an acceptable alternative to the usual traditions. From the very first she made it clear that differences of religions and/or sexual preferences made no difference. This book came about because she couldn't find any down to earth 'How to do...' training books for pagan children.

In 2019, Dolores celebrates her 90th birthday. Far from retiring, she has plans to start up a new school and has a list of books she is planning to write. She has a daughter Tamara, an acupuncturist, who also writes, and a son Carl, a retired barrister with a remarkable gift for illustrations (see the book you are holding). Dolores doesn't like being called a teacher, preferring to think of herself as a Sharer of Knowledge.

About the Illustrator

Carl Ashcroft is a retired barrister now living and working in France where he writes and illustrates children's stories. He is married to Marie-Anne Lecoeur, an expert French chic stylist. They have three grown-up children and two chihuahuas.

Also by Dolores Ashcroft Nowicki

Building a Temple
The Officers of the Temple
Your Inner Power (Sounds True: set of training CDs and Book)
The Ritual Magic Workbook
The Initiate's Book of Pathworkings
The Shining Paths
Highways of the Mind
Daughters of Eve
The New Book of the Dead
The Forgotten Mage (edited works of Kim Seymour)
Practical Magic and the Western Tradition (Edited WEBs
Lectures)
Inner Landscapes
The Sacred Cord
Illuminations
The SOL Tarot Deck
The Shakespearean Tarot Deck
The Singing Stones (Novel)
The Magical Use of Thought Forms (With JH Brennan)
My First Book of Magic
Shadows and Light (Short Stories)
The Moonboat (Poems)

Planned Works

The Hill of Dreams – Sequel to The Singing Stones (novel)
The Halls of Olympus
The Return of the Prodigal
On Looking Back (autobiography)
Tales from the Confessional (novel)

MEGALITHICA BOOKS

Books for Grownups

From our esoteric list

More details on our web site
www.immanion-press.com

Megalithica Books

IMMANION PRESS

Fiction books for adults that may be of interest to those interested in the magical, the spiritual and the occult.

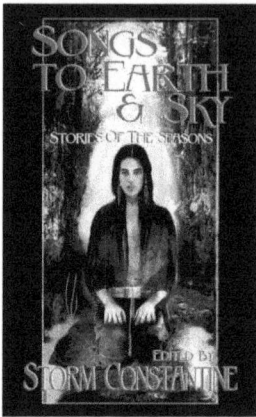

SONGS TO EARTH & SKY
STORIES OF THE SEASONS
EDITED BY STORM CONSTANTINE

THE LIGHTBEARER
Alan Richardson

The Lord of Looking-Glass
Fiona McGavin

STRINDBERG'S GHOST SONATA
and Other Uncollected Tales
TANITH LEE

More details on our web site
www.immanion-press.com

IMMANION
PRESS

Lightning Source UK Ltd.
Milton Keynes UK
UKHW010644231221
396134UK00002B/259

9 781912 241101